Our Journeys

STORIES OF HOPE, SURVIVAL, AND RESILIENCE

Learn More: www.vietnameseboatpeople.org
Email: stories@vietnameseboatpeople.org

Book designed by Katrina Schroeder, The Fiction Lab

Cover designed by Ava Wood, Fins and Feathers Designs

Artwork by Anthony Nguyen

Printed in the United States of America

ISBN: 978-1-965142-05-9 (Hardcover)
ISBN: 978-1-965142-04-2 (Paperback)
ISBN: 978-1-965142-06-6 (eBook)
LCCN: 2025903907

Published by Quill Hawk Publishing

Dedication

To my parents—thank you for your countless sacrifices and quiet strength. Your resilience and unwavering love continue to guide my purpose and the work I do with Vietnamese Boat People. Words will never capture how deeply I love you. I carry your legacy with gratitude and pride, every single day.

To our Vietnamese community, whose resilience runs deep—even when stories go unspoken—we are profoundly grateful to the individuals and families who contributed their photos and narratives to this project. Your stories honor the past, enrich the present, and ensure our legacy endures for generations to come.

From ashen fields where echoes wail,
A lotus blooms, though torn and pale.
Vietnam's heart, both land and sea,
Still beats in those who had to flee.

Through endless waves, through nights so black,
They carried home upon their backs.
Though time may fade, though scars remain,
The lotus blooms—it will not wane.

Table of Contents

Following the Fall of Saigon in 1975, nearly two million Vietnamese fled their homeland in search of freedom, braving the unknown in one of the greatest refugee crises of the 20th century.

**Yet history books
do not tell their stories.**

**Statistics have reduced their
experiences to numbers.**

**And as time passes,
their legacies risk being forgotten.**

Vietnamese Boat People nonprofit organization seeks to change that. Through personal narratives, we honor the resilience, tragedies, and triumphs of a generation that shaped the Vietnamese diaspora— ensuring that their voices endure for generations to come.

About Vietnamese Boat People

Vietnamese Boat People (VBP) is a nonprofit organization dedicated to preserving and sharing the stories of the Vietnamese diaspora. Established in 2018, our mission is to amplify these stories, educate and inspire, empower individuals to document their histories, and foster meaningful connections.

The organization's name, Vietnamese Boat People (VBP), initially paid tribute to the millions of refugees who fled Vietnam by boat. Since then, the organization has evolved and is dedicated to supporting all stories from the Vietnamese diaspora community. Through innovative storytelling, digital archives, and community-driven programs, we provide accessible platforms for communities to engage with these narratives. Our award-winning Vietnamese Boat People podcast sheds light on untold, first-person stories spanning multiple generations. VBP has been recognized by Forbes, Apple Podcasts, PRX, Google, National Geographic, NPR affiliates, and critical refugee studies worldwide. To learn more, visit www.vietnameseboatpeople.org.

Our Journeys

Our Journeys is a collection of personal stories gathered by the Vietnamese Boat People (VBP) organization. Rooted in lived experiences of displacement, migration, and resilience, this anthology centers our community as the narrators of our own histories—past and present.

Created to accompany the *Our Journeys* exhibition presented by VBP, this book deepens the themes explored in the exhibit. Divided into three parts—Endurance and Flight, Adaptation and Identity, and Intergenerational Impact & Moving Forward—it offers more than a series of narratives and photographs. It is an invitation to bear witness, to remember, and to reflect. Within these pages are testaments to survival, love, and hope passed down through generations—and to the enduring spirit that binds us, even in the face of loss and change.

The narratives and images in this book were graciously shared by members of our community through an open call for submissions. Each story portrays a deeply personal and intergenerational journey that spans time, geography, and memory. Please note that names and narratives have been preserved as submitted—some include diacritics, others do not. Together, they illuminate the strength, complexity, and humanity of the Vietnamese diaspora.

Preface

In 1981, just before my fourth birthday, my mother orchestrated our escape from Vietnam's communist rule. With nothing but the clothes on our backs, she led my two older sisters and me—three little girls under the age of ten—and our teenage cousin through the dense jungle in the dead of night before boarding a fragile, wooden fishing boat with strangers.

For two years, my eldest sister, only ten, dreamed of the day we would reunite with our father and brothers, who had fled Vietnam before us. I was too young to share that dream—I had no memories of them, only the life we were leaving behind.

The shadows of war, escape, and displacement shaped our family in profound, lasting ways. Growing up, I felt the weight of all that was unspoken. I watched my parents work multiple jobs to make ends meet. My mother sacrificed the most, taking on extra work to provide for our family, put my father through community college, and support the relatives we left behind in Vietnam.

On the days we saw our mother, she shared beautiful moments of her upbringing in Vietnam. But the remembrances of war and a fallen country quickly overshadowed those memories. She recounted the painful stories of living in post-1975 Vietnam—a past filled with hardship and loss. I didn't want to listen; the stories made me incredibly sad, and I found it easier to run away from them.

In America, my four older brothers struggled to fit in and find their way in a world so different from the one we left behind, while my sisters and I leaned on each other for comfort. In the absence of our parents, our eldest sister carried the heavy burden of being a parent, sibling, and friend to her two younger sisters.

We each navigated our lives differently, silently struggling with our internal battles. We instinctively knew to endure it and do whatever we could to survive in this new country without burdening our parents. Much of my adolescence was spent feeling lost and out of place.

It was only when I had children of my own that I began to take an interest in my family's story. As I unraveled the layers, I began to reconcile with the sacrifices and trauma that my family had endured, and I finally appreciated our history and resilience. This journey led me to create the Vietnamese Boat People (VBP) nonprofit organization to honor the stories of my family and others who fled Vietnam, faced uncertainty, and rebuilt their lives from nothing.

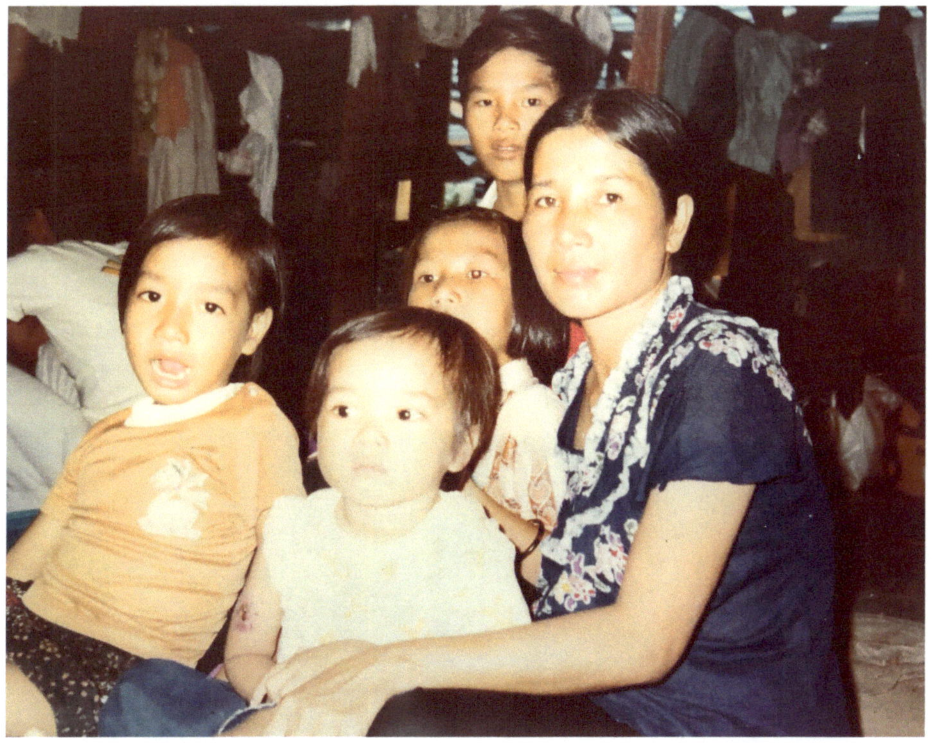

Tracey and her family in their tent at the Singapore Refugee Camp at Hawkins Road. On Tracey's right arm is a vaccination shot that left a scar to this day. From left to right: her sister JoAnh, Tracey (in white), her mom Mary, behind is her sister Tu Anh and her cousin Khanh.

Tracey and her mom on a plane from Hawkins Road refugee camp in Singapore to America.

Reunited with her brothers after two years of separation, at the airport in Louisiana; her father is taking the photo. (1981)

Since 2018, VBP has had the privilege of collecting stories from our diaspora community through various programming. We believe in the transformative power of storytelling to empower individuals, foster healing, and build connections that transcend generations and borders.

The Vietnamese refugee story is not just history—it is a legacy carried forward by those who listen, learn, and share. As you turn these pages, may the vignettes serve as powerful reminders that the refugee story is not just a distant past—it's a living reality for millions today. Through these captured moments, I hope you recognize that displacement and the search for freedom continue across the world. By honoring these stories, we reaffirm our shared humanity and our collective responsibility to offer compassion and support to those still seeking safety and dignity.

With gratitude,
Tracey Nguyễn Mang (Nguyễn Quán Trường-Anh)
Founder, Vietnamese Boat People

Tracey with her mom and sisters in Louisiana, one year after resettlement. (1982)

Endurance
and Flight

To stay was pain, to leave was death,
Yet freedom called with fleeting breath.
Through jungle depths, on restless waves,
They gambled all, their lives they gave.

"I was four or five years old when he [Dad] was sent to reeducation labor camp. It was just myself and two sisters staying behind with my mother. I remember that we didn't have enough to eat. So my grandparents from my father's side had decided to help her out by taking me. And I remember leaving the family. It was probably one of the saddest points in my life there, the family being split apart at that moment."

LISTEN HERE

"This is one of the only photos I have of my dad (Kiểm Duy Trịnh) from his time in the navy. I don't know if this was before or after his capture, but I am guessing it was before. The only story he told me about his capture was that he collected rain water on leaves and saved salt to share with his unit when they were all captured. He rationed all his food to help keep them alive. This photo makes me sad and proud of my dad."

———————————————

THẢO-CHÂU TRỊNH

Kiểm Duy Trịnh (on the left) and his band of Navy brothers.

"This was the last school year before the North Vietnamese communists took over the south. In principle, graduates were given a temporary degree and then an official degree, but in the end, they were not awarded an official degree because the North Vietnamese communists did not recognize the pharmacy program trained by the Republic of Vietnam.

The new pharmacists who graduated that year faced many difficulties in finding jobs. Some had to quit their jobs and return to their hometowns to work in the new economic zones, some worked without pay for a long time but still had to stick around to avoid being sent to work in the new economic zones, and others went abroad. Pharmacy students scattered like many other people after 1975."

HUỲNH T. THANH NHÀN

Huỳnh Thị Thanh Nhan (third from the left in the dark áo dài) with fellow pharmacy students by the school fountain in Saigon. (1973)

"This photo was taken before I was born—I'm guessing around 1969. I see my parents, so young and in love, full of hopes and dreams even as their beloved homeland was waging a civil war.

My mom was 19 years old when she gave birth to me—just over a year after losing her firstborn baby boy. A threat against doctors had forced her caregivers to stay away from the hospital the day my brother, Anh Hai, was born. He lived less than a week as my aunts desperately searched for a healthcare provider who could help. My mother nearly died because she had lost so much blood. She was barely 18 years old."

———————————————————————

LƯU TRỌNG ĐẠ THẢO (TINA LƯU)

Luu Trong Tuong and Le Thi Hanh in Vietnam.

The family outside the refugee tent at Camp Pendleton. (1975)

"When our family arrived that May, Pentagon records showed Camp Pendleton had 18,000 Vietnamese living in eight 'tent cities.' Our family of seven was assigned to city No. 8, tent 88, which we shared with several other families."

NOELANI TANITA

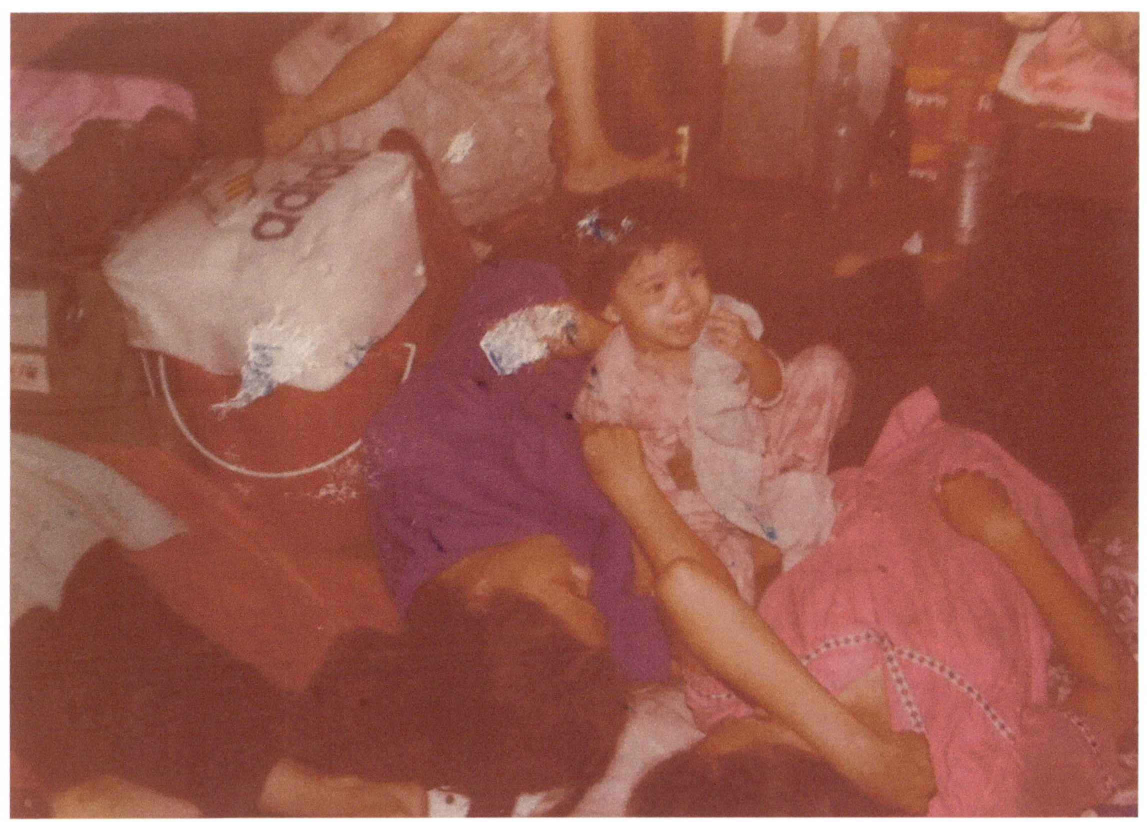

Theresa Mei Chuc (child) with her mother (in pink) and aunt (in blue) aboard a Vietnamese refugee freight boat in the East Sea. (1978)

"In the photo, we were on a refugee boat escaping Vietnam. I was two years old, crying and sitting in between my mother (wearing pick) and my auntie (wearing blue) who were both lying on the ground.

My father was taken away to a Vietcong reeducation camp, and conditions were terrible for my family. I grew up without a father for the first nine years of my life because he was in a reeducation camp in Vietnam. Dealing with the trauma when he was finally released was one of our greatest challenges as refugees. My parents worked very hard in minimum-wage jobs to help us survive and put food on the table for my brother and me."

THERESA MEI CHUC

"I am incredibly proud of my mom, Thu Cuc Nguyen, and her perseverance to flee her homeland without her family. She landed in the midwest, found work, built a family, worked multiple jobs, and eventually graduated from nursing school in the United States at fifty years old.

This is my mother wearing fashionable clothes that she was proud to buy on her own after moving to Saigon to work for a large bank. She grew up one of ten children on a farm in Da Nang and always had aspirations to become a business woman in the city."

———————————————

AUDREY NGUYEN BRYANT

Thu Cuc Nguyen at age 22 in Saigon, Vietnam. (February 1972)

Four generations of women at Camp Pendleton.

"This picture is of my mother, Dr. Carolee Tran (on the far left), next to her is her maternal great grandmother (second from the left), maternal grandmother (second from the right), three of her sisters and her mother (at the top) at Camp Pendleton, the refugee camp where they spent months waiting for resettlement. My great grandmother (in the brown áo dài) looks distraught as she had just received news that one of her sons, who was a fighter pilot in the Southern Vietnamese military, had been captured by the communists. He was imprisoned for ten years and was never able to see my great grandmother again. He was able to make it to America in 1991."

CARINA KIMLAN HINTON

"My father, Võ Thành Long, was a helicopter pilot in the South Vietnam Air Force based in Đà Nẵng. We had to leave to avoid being put into reeducation camps at the end of the war. He had to ditch his helicopter in the ocean after dropping us off on the USS Oklahoma City. My mother, Trương Hoàng Vân, was pregnant during the exodus. My sister, Võ Hoàng Ly Hương, was born prematurely in Camp Pendleton but did not survive past six weeks. She was given a Catholic service, though my family is Buddhist."

CONG VO

The Võ family attending a funeral service at Eternal Hills Mortuary in Oceanside, CA mourning the loss of their six-week old baby girl who was born in the Camp Pendleton refugee camp. (1975)

Trương Hoàng Vân on the day of the funeral. Eternal Hills Mortuary, Oceanside, CA. (1975)

"I love this photo of my dad so much because it captures the incredible strength and resilience he showed during one of the hardest chapters of our family's journey. He survived seven days at sea alongside my mom and my one-year-old sister, helping to organize a boat for 400 people to escape Vietnam. Their boat was hijacked by pirates, yet they survived and eventually made it to the refugee camp.

This photo signifies such an important part of their story—a moment of profound courage and hope. It marks the beginning of a journey of starting over, again and again, in pursuit of a better life for us all."

———————————————————————

NANCY LUONG

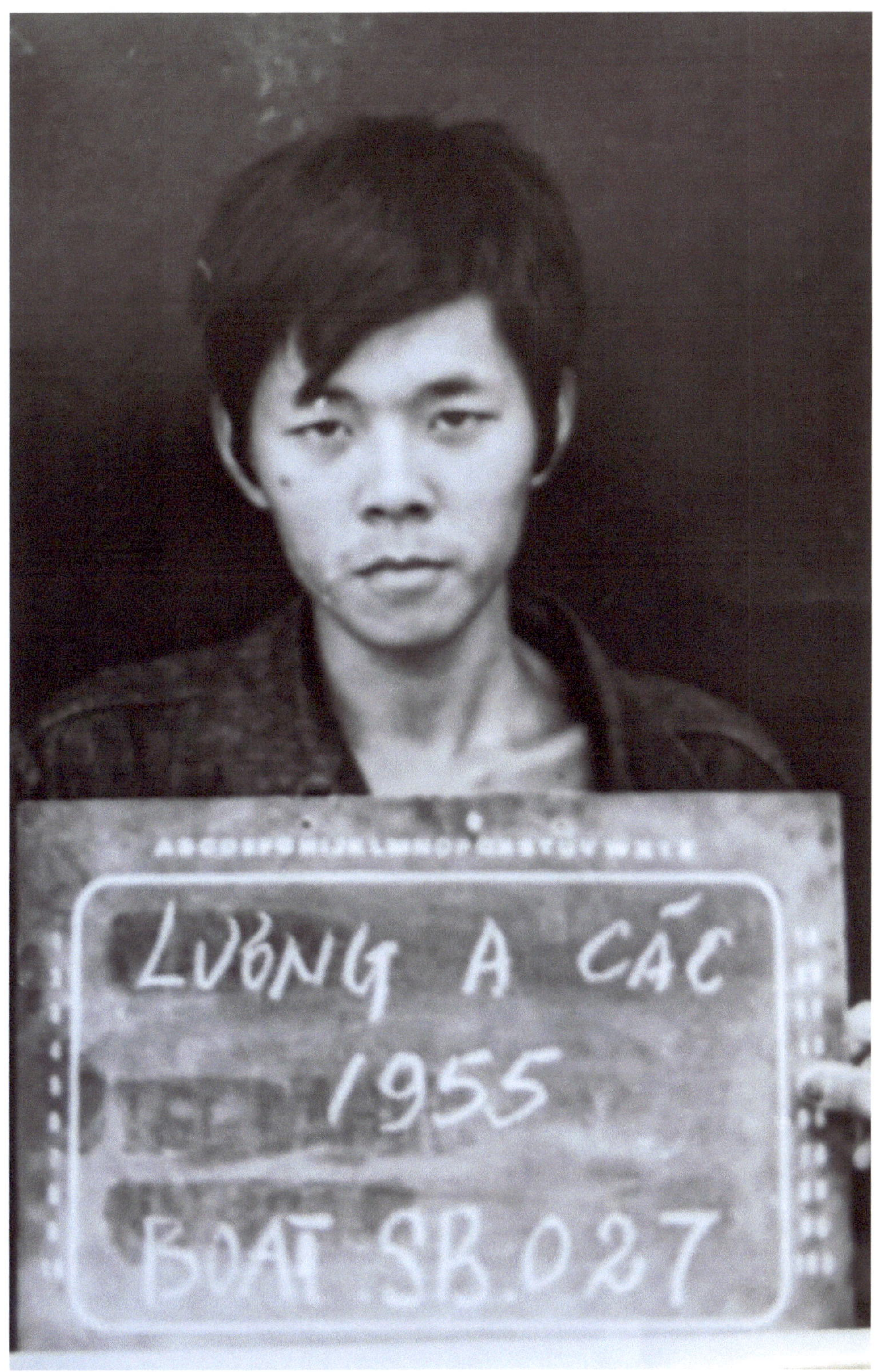

Nancy's Dad, Cac Luong, ID photo taken at the refugee camp when he first got to Indonesia.

"A family who had that fruit stand was granted a place to go live so they gave this fruit stand to my mom as a gift. Their hope was that my mom could take over to earn money to survive. My parents lived in the refugee camp for two years."

———————————————

NANCY LUONG

Nancy's mom, Nguyet Truong, and sister selling fruit at the Galang Refugee Camp in Indonesia. (1979)

Crystal Ngo's parents as a young couple arriving in Virginia as new immigrants. (1987)

"My parents did not know each other in Vietnam; they met at a refugee camp in Malaysia. After they decided to get married, my mom split from her family and joined my dad to come to America together. I asked if it was scary to start a new life in a new country, and my parents always said, 'Nothing could be harder than what we left.' This picture was taken the day they arrived in America, ready to start again."

CRYSTAL NGO

Kim Oanh Le (left) with a friend at their English class graduation party at the Galang Refugee Camp in Indonesia.

"I was mostly separated from my family after leaving Vietnam. That was the last time we were all together. I was sent to a refugee camp in Galang, Indonesia and later relocated to Pulau Kuku, Malaysia. There was also the language barrier that continues to be a challenge for me to this day. When I came to the states, I didn't have my family or a community who could support me.

This was me graduating out of a level of English class. We held a graduation party for all the graduates at the refugee camp in Galang."

KIM OANH LE

"In 1989, I left Vietnam on a small fishing boat and traveled to Hong Kong. I lived in Whitehead Detention Centre, a large camp for Vietnamese refugees, until 1997. In 1992, I began working as a teacher for the young children growing up in Whitehead. I loved my students, and teaching gave me something meaningful to do during the many years I spent in Hong Kong. One of the boys in my class moved to the U.S. with his family, while all my other students were repatriated to Vietnam and remain there to this day."

KHUE NGUYEN

Khue Nguyen with her second grade students at Whitehead Detention Centre in Hong Kong. (1996)

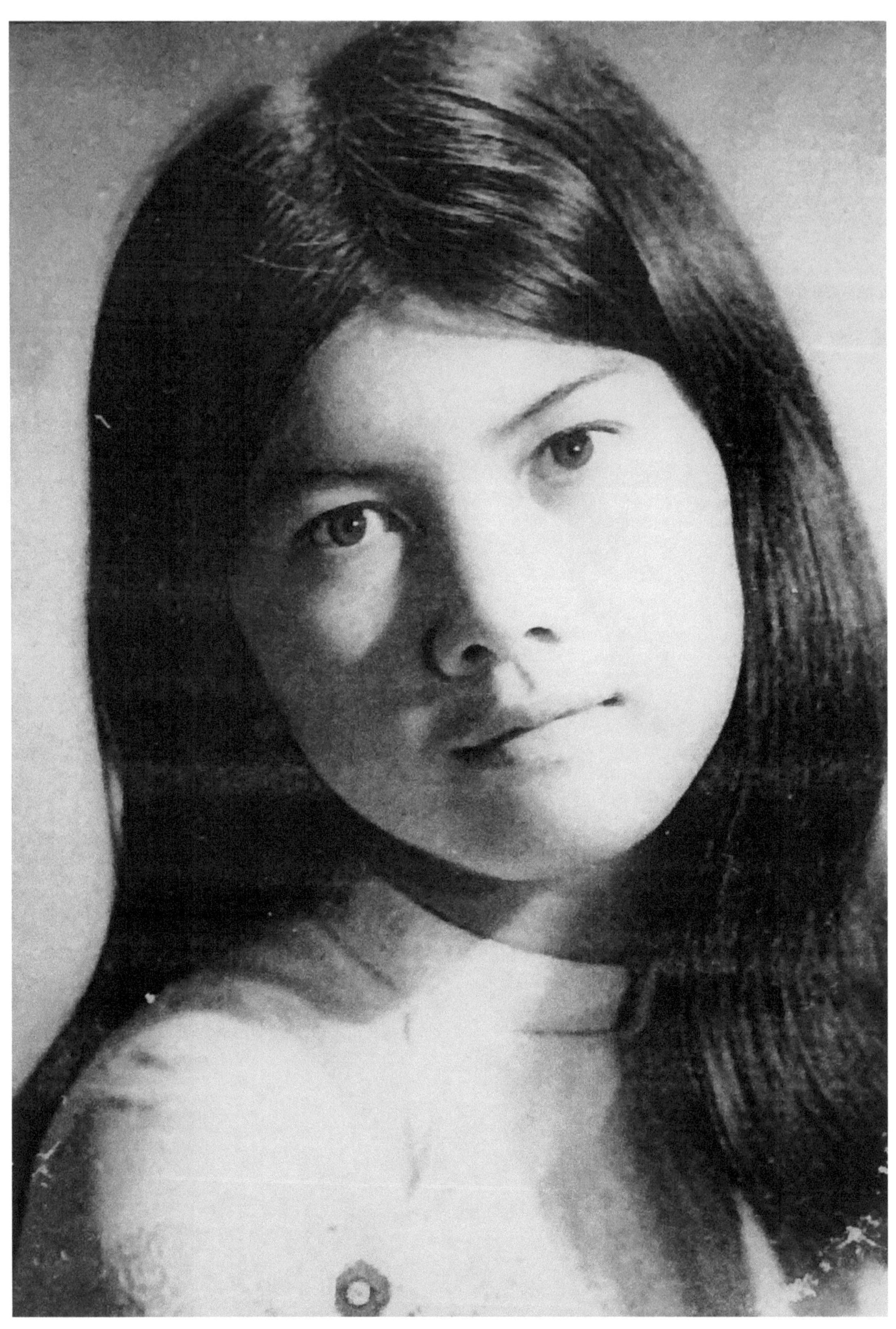

Nguyễn Thị Bích Thu, 1957–1983

"In 1983, my mother's youngest sister, Nguyễn Thị Bích Thu, attempted to flee Vietnam with her two children, ages five and seven. My mother was already in America by then, holding onto the hope that they would be reunited. But just one day out at sea, a big storm came and the boat capsized. There was only one survivor.

It would be several months before my mother learned what had happened. The man who survived tried to find our family, tracing connections through old friends and neighbors until, miraculously, he reached ours. Dì Thu (Aunt Thu) had swum with all her strength, one child in each arm—but all she had were her legs. He begged her to hold onto his back, and for a time, she tried. But she couldn't let go of her children. And as the waves crashed around them, he turned back—and in the darkness they were gone.

My mother says Dì Thu was a gifted musician—kind, beautiful, and smart. She says I look like her. I don't know if that's true, but when she speaks of an aunt I never knew, I feel both her love and her loss. I'm honored to be a reminder of her baby sister."

TRACEY NGUYỄN MANG

"My parents, An Van Trieu and Nguyet Phuong, escaped Vietnam in 1978. Along with 416 other refugees, they were rescued miraculously in the South China Sea by the USS Whipple on August 22, 1978. After they were rescued, they married in a church in Hong Kong; their story was dubbed as a 'love story at sea.'

My parents celebrated 46 years of marriage in 2024. Since then, they have spent a majority of their lives in Pennsylvania and have traveled the world, serving their community through haircuts and food via their salon and restaurant businesses, creating communities with their local church, and continually making a lifetime of memories with their friends, three children, five grandchildren, and large extended family. Their drive to succeed, commitment to hard work, and compassion for others have led them to truly live the American Dream."

JANE TRIEU

An Van Trieu and Nguyet Phuong on their engagement day in Vietnam.

An Van Trieu and Nguyet Phuong on their wedding day in Hong Kong. (1978)

Chương Khôi Liên was in a reeducation camp in Vietnam from 1975-1977.

The metal comb that Chương Khôi Liên made in reeducation camp for his wife.

"My father, Chương Khôi Liên, fought in the war for the South Vietnamese navy as a naval lieutenant. While in a prison camp for former military officers and supporters of the South Vietnamese government, he made this comb for my Má (mother). Metal from a fallen plane was used to create this gift. He worked on filing the comb each evening. To avoid the guards confiscating it, he would bury it in the dirt. During his two-year imprisonment, Má was able to visit one time. This was when the comb was secretly given to her. The comb has been in my possession since December of 2004, the month when Má passed away."

PHƯƠNG LIÊN PALAFOX

"After 1975 and the fall of Saigon, our family was accused of being criminals because of our wealth and our mixed heritage (part Chinese). The communist regime took all our property, money, and everything we owned. We were forced to leave Saigon and relocate to an underdeveloped, rural countryside.

This is a portrait of my family. I left behind my mom and siblings. I was the first one to successfully escape to a refugee camp in Malaysia. My two older brothers tried to leave first, but both got caught and sent to jail.

I did not speak the language. I had no trade or skill for a job as I wasn't able to finish school in Vietnam. I had no money. I lost everything. I left Vietnam by myself and did not have any family or friends. I look back now and do not know how I made it. I am surprised to have survived. I cannot feel proud of anything; I just feel lucky."

HÚA THANH TÂN

A family portrait taken in the An Lạc ward of Bình Chánh, a rural district southwest of Saigon, Vietnam. (1982) Not pictured are Hứa Thanh Tân and his two older brothers.

"This is the only photo of my parents in Vietnam that still exists. Even though they lived during a two-decades long war, this photo captures a glimpse of their lives independent of the war. It captures the beauty of when they fell in love. My parents had to leave their extended family and home country, and navigate a different language and system, to create a new life for themselves. They redefined home away from home."

JULIE MAI TRAN

Julie Tran's parents dating in Vietnam. (1974)

"My mother, Vũ Thị Phượng, told me that twenty-one people shared the temporary structure that our family lived in. At night, everyone laid on the floor, side by side, in two rows, feet towards the wall and heads in the center line. There was one window in the structure, and a man who made himself the keeper of that window, did not allow the window to be opened. It was extremely stuffy in there.

My mother had no chairs to sit on with her very pregnant belly. She sat on the floor in the relentless summer heat, sewing shirts for other refugees for five Hong Kong dollars a shirt. In the evenings when it got dark, she went outside for fresh air. When she went inside to sleep, she tiptoed so as to not step on people's heads."

———————————————

TERRY NGO

Vũ Thị Phượng and her family in a temporary structure home shared with multiple families at Camp David in Hong Kong. (June 1975)

Ngô Thế Hưng and his son, Ngô Phương Hải, at Camp David in Hong Kong. (June 1975)

"Our family left Vietnam because our father was in the South Vietnamese Army and didn't want to go to reeducation camp. Our parents lived under communism in the north for a time and suffered greatly. Although it was a struggle, this photo shows that my father, Ngô Thế Hưng, and my older brother, Ngô Phương Hải, were happy to have each other and survived the journey on the boat."

TERRY NGO

Loan Thị Kiều Hứa and Phương Thanh Nguyễn on their wedding day in Westminster, CA. (January 20, 1990)

"We were neighbors who became best friends in Ba Ria - Vung Tau. We reunited after escaping Vietnam in Westminster, California. This photo was taken on our wedding day, in our first apartment on Bolsa Avenue. This beautiful day felt like the start of a new life toward achieving the American Dream, filled with opportunities, hope, and love."

LOAN THỊ KIỀU HỨA, PHƯƠNG THANH NGUYỄN

Trực Nguyễn poses for his first photo on American soil at the Camp Pendleton refugee camp in San Diego.

"On April 28, 1975, my father, Trực Nguyễn, flew on an all-day mission to Phu Quoc Island to deliver supplies. He returned from his mission with a barrel of the famous Phu Quoc Fish Sauce that my grandma requested. As rockets continued to fire in the distance, my father knew it was time to leave again, but he didn't want to tell his family. He put all of his documents, money, and photos into a purple bag my grandfather tailored. My father told his family he had to return to Tan Son Nhut Air Base to ensure everything was okay since he was one of the squadron leaders.

He jumped on his moped and hurried back to base. Upon arrival, he was immediately injured during a rocket attack and sustained a leg injury. After getting stitched up in the field, he knew he had to leave because there would be no way out if the airbase and runway got damaged. Along with comrades and civilians nearby, he boarded his cargo plane and departed from Tan Son Nhut. He would not step foot back in his homeland for another 25+ years."

TUẤN NGUYỄN

"After my father left on April 29, 1975, his family assumed he was dead. One of his brothers had gone into Tan Son Nhut Air Base after the rocket attacks to find my father. When he came to his plane hangar, my uncle saw my father's moped covered in blood, so he assumed the worst. It wasn't until three years later that my father contacted a relative in France who was able to relay back to his family in Vietnam that he was alive and living in the United States, specifically Seattle, Washington. This picture was the first family photo taken in Vietnam to send to my father to inspire him to gain US citizenship and sponsor each family member. It took many years, but he was successful in doing so."

TUẤN NGUYỄN

The Nguyễn Family in Saigon, Vietnam (1979)

Đặng Dân Nam with his wife, Phuoc, on their wedding day in Saigon.
(1971)

"Back in the day, many soldiers got married and immediately went to war. This photo was taken the day I married my wife, Phước. It was the happiest day of my life. The next day, instead of going on our honeymoon, I returned to the battlefield."

ĐẶNG DÂN NAM

"1985 was a year that I would never ever forget in my entire life. I lost my younger sister, lost my father, and our lives completely changed. I never felt that I was the same again."

"Soldiers have many responsibilities, but they must also have times of relaxation and enjoyment with their fellow soldiers. This photo was taken right after a tour in enemy territory. We did not know if we would return, but we did. We celebrated as Vietnamese do... with beer, cigarettes, and our favorite drinking foods.

I was a lieutenant in the Army of the Republic of Vietnam Special Forces (Lực Lượng Đặc Biệt Lôi Hổ) and spent seven years in a re-education camp. Even after I was released, I, along with other ARVN soldiers, was still seen as the enemy. My family and I were closely watched and harassed. We were not allowed to live in the city and had to move to the wilderness. My children were not allowed to apply to university, and I knew they would not have the life I dreamed of for them if we stayed in Vietnam. On my mother-in-law's deathbed, she made me promise that I would take our family and move to the United States in hopes of a better future for my children. Thanks to the U.S. government's Humanitarian Operation (HO) settlement program, I was able to leave the only home I had ever known behind, and my family started over in the United States with nothing but each other — and freedom."

———————————————

ĐẶNG DÂN NAM

Đặng Dân Nam (right) with a comrade at the Marine Corps training center. (1970)

"My dad, Frank Luong, escaped on his own. However, he found a family with the people he escaped with, pictured here. They were all brothers and sisters and took my dad in as if he was their own brother. Their boat was sinking in international waters; fortunately, they were saved by a Japanese cargo ship and ended up in Japan before he found his way to the US."

―――――――――――――――――――――――――――――――――――

THERESA LUONG

Frank Luong (top row, second to right) with his family of boatmates in Japan. (1970s)

Brian (Duy) Hoang with his parents in Saigon, Vietnam. (1979)

"This is a photo of my ba and mẹ (parents) with their first child (me). They are in their mid-late 20's in this picture, taken four years after the end of the war. We lived in Saigon close to all our extended family. Two years from this moment, almost all of us would make our escape to a refugee camp."

Brian (Duy) Hoang with his parents at the Galang Refugee Camp in Indonesia. (1982)

"In 1981, we were able to flee out of Vietnam on our second attempt. Our boat journey was relatively problem-free compared to many others' journeys. After about seven days out at sea, we made it to the Galang Refugee Camp where we spent the next six months until my parents and I were sponsored to Canada in 1982 (with the rest of my family making it to the U.S. shortly after)."

BRIAN (DUY) HOANG

"The day that Saigon fell on April 30, 1975, my dad was studying in America while my mom and sister were in Saigon.

In 1975, when South Vietnam lost the war, my mom and sister got stuck, and they lost contact with my dad.

After the south lost, my mom burned every picture, every letter, every piece of documentation connecting her to my dad for fear of what would happen to her and my sister if the Viet Cong knew who my dad was. Eventually, they escaped as boat people in 1978.

This picture exists only because my dad brought it with him to Nashville, TN in 1973."

———————————————————

ANHTUAN DO

The only remaining wedding picture of Anhtuan Do's parents on their wedding day in Saigon.
(1970)

"This little fishing boat is overcrowded with 124 Vietnamese boat people. My dad and uncle are among the crowd. My dad is standing at the back of the boat. Many others had no energy to keep upright and lay down at the front of the trawler, lethargic from starvation yet still alive. The rescue crew aboard the MV Ruddbank took this photo."

____

MEGGIE TRAN

This little wooden fishing trawler carried 124 Vietnamese boat people across the South China Sea, northwest of Borneo. (1979)

This little wooden fishing trawler carried 124 Vietnamese boat people across the South China Sea. (1979)

"These photos were taken at the UNHCR refugee camp in Songkhla, Thailand. My father, Hưng Quốc Lê, was the skipper of the boat.

On the back of one of the photos is a note written by my mother, Nguyệt Thanh Phạm. She wrote it to her parents after arriving in Songkhla. She missed her family very much. The note reads:

'Songkhla 10.02.1980 Miss you Mom and Dad. This is the first photo I have. My boatmates took a souvenir photo in front of the Songkhla refugee camp where I am currently residing. You still haven't changed, right, Mom? I'm sad and miss my family so much (let me kiss Khanh ten times, miss and obey your grandparents, Khanh), Nguyệt'"

—————————————————————————

ANNESTA LE

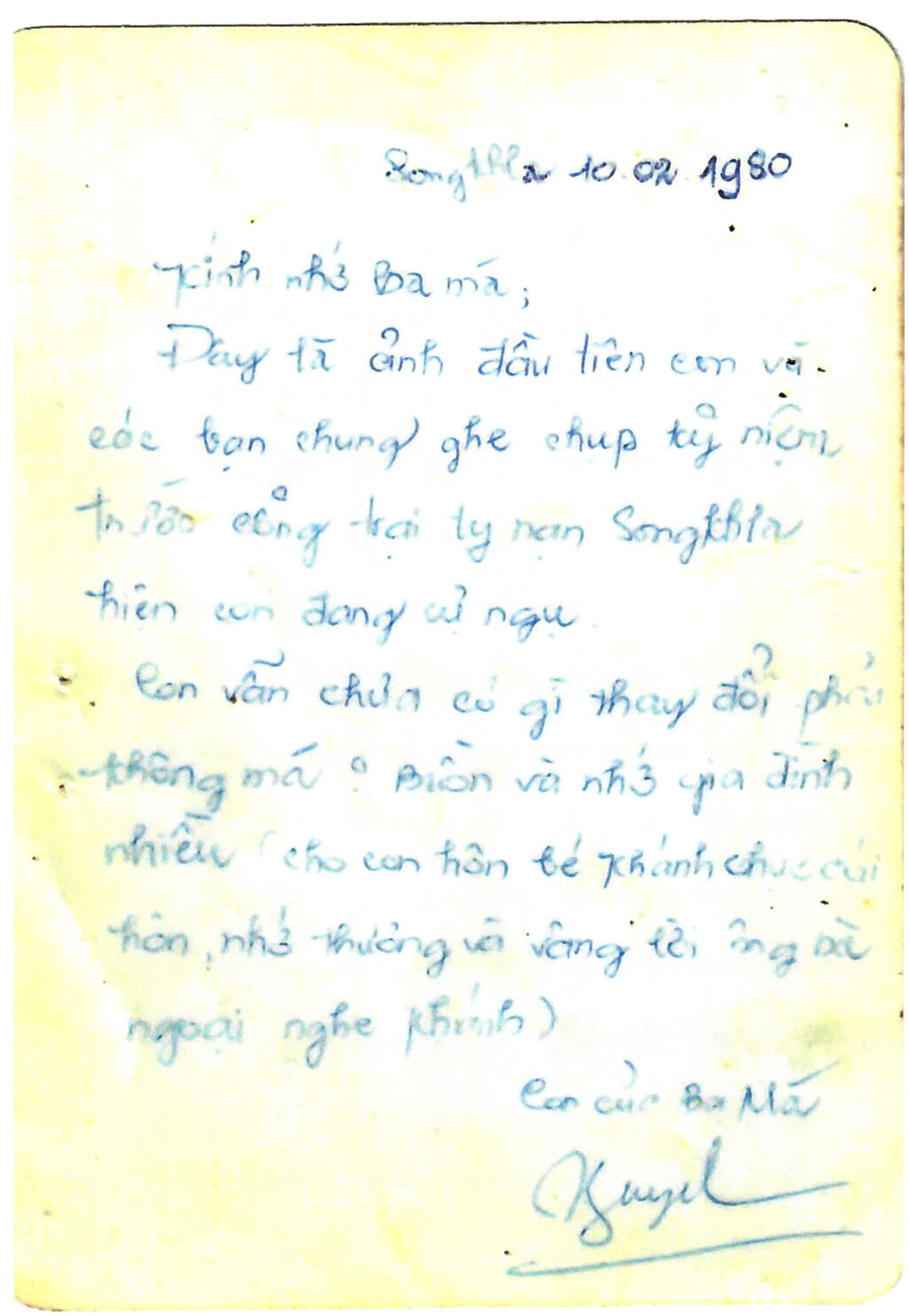

A note written on the back of a photo by Nguyệt Thanh Phạm to her parents while she was at the refugee camp in Songkhla, Thailand. (October 1980)

Annesta's parents, Hung Quốc Lê (front center) and his wife, Nguyệt Thanh Phạm (second row, center), with fellow refugees at the UNHCR camp in Songkhla, Thailand. (1980)

Annesta's father, Hung Quốc Lê (standing) teaches an English class at the UNHCR refugee camp of Songkhla, Thailand.

"My painting envisions a sky full of stars, each one representing an ancestor looking over our families and guiding them on the journey to safety. I painted the China Sea being covered by jewels beyond our belief, each treasure representing those that didn't survive the journey. I almost died leaving Vietnam since I was malnourished and connected to an intravenous tube the moment I arrived at the refugee camp in Malaysia. I was five months old when our family left. This painting spawned a very personal conversation with my mother (who had kept much of the war and her life in Vietnam a secret). I think she kept her sad stories close to her heart, because she was traumatised and wanted to protect me from any shame, guilt, or grief she felt."

AN NGUYEN

A painting by An Nguyen titled "Hopes Adrift," demonstrating the perilous journey from Vietnam to freedom. (Ottawa, Canada - 2024)

"'My wife and I have a family of seven children. By American standards, that's a lot, but by Vietnamese standards, it's perfectly acceptable. We married in 1960, and in the years that followed, we started with four sons in a row. In a society where boys are preferred over girls—like in most Asian countries—people believed that having four sons in a row would bring prosperity and good luck to the family. I don't know if we ever had any particular good luck, but we wished for a daughter—and we were blessed with three daughters in a row.'"

FRANK SANH NGUYỄN

Frank Sanh Nguyễn and his wife, Mary Liễu Nguyễn, on their wedding day in Nha Trang Vietnam.
(1960)

"'Tú Anh was the first on our wish list. Next came JoAnh (Giang Anh), who was born just as South Vietnam was about to fall to the communists in 1975. Our family was forced to evacuate our hometown of Đà Nẵng when JoAnh was three days old. It was a time of war—destruction, chaos, and death was everywhere. Maybe it's the hard times that make a newborn stronger later in life. Then came Tracey (Trường Anh), our seventh child; she was very independent at an early age. She had to be… when you're the seventh child, there isn't much room for extra attention—especially not in the post-war conditions of Vietnam that Tracey was born into.'

(An excerpt from a toast delivered on the wedding day of my youngest daughter Tracey.)"

FRANK SANH NGUYỄN

Frank and Mary's three daughters at the refugee camp in
Hawkins Road in Singapore. (1981) Left to right: Tú Anh,
Tracey (Trường Anh), JoAnh (Giang Anh)

Frank and Mary's four sons in Louisiana. (1981) Left to right: Steve (Tuấn Anh), Rocky (Quốc
Anh), Chris (Bảo Anh), Danny (Phúc Anh)

"My father painstakingly crafted this replica of the boat we escaped on as 'boat people' fleeing the Vietnam War. For him, this boat is a tribute to the hardships he endured and the sacrifices he made to secure a brighter future for our family. It's his way of preserving our story, honoring the courage it took to leave everything behind, and ensuring that future generations understand the strength it required to rebuild our lives. The boat, much like my father, carries an unspoken legacy of resilience, love, and an unbreakable determination to rise above even the greatest of challenges."

CELINA TRAN

Celina Tran"s father presenting a tribute of a handcrafted boat that carried the family to freedom (Macon, GA - 1981)

Dang Thi Phi (left) with the staff at a medical clinic in the Pulau Tengah refugee camp of Malaysia. (Fall 1978)

"As a trained doctor in Vietnam, my mother, Đặng Thị Phỉ, was pulled into service at the medical clinic at Pulau Tengah refugee camp in Malaysia, where she had landed as a boat person in August 1978. She spent three months at the camp (August-November 1978) before being resettled in Florida, where her eldest sibling was living after having escaped Vietnam in April 1975."

ANH THƯ NGUYỄN

"They don't let me contact the family or anything [in reeducation camp]. My mom went looking for me, she said, I believe my son is still alive. When they finally released me, I was 22 years old. I returned home, and the first time she saw me, she said, 'I knew it, I knew it. You come home.' Then she asked, 'Are you hungry?"

QUANG TRAN
THE PERFECT STORM
EPISODE 24
VIETNAMESE BOAT PEOPLE PODCAST

LISTEN HERE

Adaptation
and Identity

Far from home, yet not alone,
In stories told, their roots have grown.
Between two worlds, they carve their space,
Finding belonging, finding place.

"When I got older and I saw my mother in this new environment and she was being mistreated, I wanted to preserve her ignorance in a way, because she didn't understand English, and there were these people who were just yelling at her or calling her these racial slurs that she didn't understand."

LY TRAN
HOUSE OF STICKS
EPISODE 38
VIETNAMESE BOAT PEOPLE PODCAST

LISTEN HERE

"We were forced out. We didn't leave Vietnam, we escaped Vietnam. My search for love and acceptance amid poverty turned my youth into a comedy of errors, leading me to a dangerous gang experience that threatened to tear my life apart.

I wrote I Love Yous Are for White People, a heart-wrenching, irreverent, and ultimately uplifting, memoir depicting the struggles that countless individuals faced in their quest to belong and endure in pursuit of a father's fleeting affection."

LAC SU

"This was my kindergarten graduation picture in Louisiana. My mom looked absolutely stunning in her áo dài and sunglasses, a picture of grace and elegance. She made sure I had something decent to wear. She looked through all the secondhand clothing stores and church donation bins for something that would help me fit in with the rest of the American kids. Even though I was young, I could see how much she cared about making sure I was accepted, and that love and effort still stays with me today."

JOANH PITTS

JoAnh Pitts with her mother in Chalmette, Louisiana on the day of JoAnh's graduation from kindergarten.

Hoàng Thi Hương (left) and Lê Quang Tuyến (right) together at Chickamauga Lake in Chattanooga, TN. (October 23, 1977)

"This is a photo of my parents, Hoàng Thi Hương (age 23) and Lê Quang Tuyến (age 26), at Chickamauga Lake on October 23, 1977 after moving to Chattanooga, TN, where my family still resides."

———————————————

ANTHONY LE

Nancy Le Blair (baby) with her paåçrents and brother at the Le Family Baptism in Houston, TX. (1980)

"It took my parents seven years after arriving in the US before they decided they were capable of taking care of another child. I was born only because my parents were more financially secure, had dedicated childcare, and my older brother was old enough to help out at home. It was an incredible act of mindfulness and consideration for my parents to wait so long after fleeing Vietnam."

NANCY LE BLAIR

"In this photo, my mother stands in front of the Singapore refugee camp Hawkins Road before relocating to the Vietnamese refugee camp in Bataan, Philippines. In gratitude for the country that saved them, she would later name her baby Sinh, after Singapore—a tribute to the place that gave our family a second chance at life.

Growing up in a first-generation Vietnamese household in East Oakland, in the heart of the hood, meant making the most of what we had. Gunshots often masked themselves as fireworks, and sideshows in the streets were our weekend entertainment. We didn't have much, but we had enough. We had our parents to show us how to survive anything, anywhere.

For a long time, I fought with my parents about how Americanized I had become in their household. Yet, at school, I was too Asian and suffered a lot of racism throughout my grade school experience."

———————————————

SINH LE

Sinh Le's mother, Diep Banh, in front of the Hawkins Road refugee camp in Singapore. (1987)

The Le Family (Sinh is second to left) in Oakland, California. (1997)

Toon at age five enjoying his first bowl of pho in the US in Oklahoma City, OK. (January 1981)

"We spent so many Thanksgivings and Christmases in America, just the two of us. Mom would cry her heart out, and as a kid, I'd try to do something funny to make her laugh. We'd laugh, then go back to crying.

This is a photo of the first time I had pho and it would also be the last time as I was allergic to star anise, one of the primary ingredients in this delicious Vietnamese beef noodle soup!"

THUẬN "TOON" HIẾU NGUYỄN

Portrait of Toon's father and siblings, taken in Saigon during Tết (Vietnamese Lunar New Year), with a framed photo their mother had sent from America.

Tam Le (bottom right in the pink shirt) at a birthday party for her cousin, Kristi Vo (bottom row second from the right in the birthday crown), in Houston, TX. (1996)

"I was flipping through old photos and saw this one of my cousins and I celebrating a birthday. I was struck by the glee on our faces and how unabashedly joyful we were. At that time my cousins were my only friends and it didn't matter that we looked different. We didn't worry about whether we were Vietnamese or Vietnamese Americans. We just were."

TÂM LÊ

Young mothers with their children in Indonesia. (1984-1985)

"The split between two cultures and not fitting in with either has been my biggest challenge. It has been an emotional struggle for me personally. The trauma has stayed with me and is overwhelming every time I think about my mom and what she must have felt with two small children on her hip.

My mother is an amazingly strong and beautiful woman—a devoted mother and wife, and now the best grandmother. She doesn't get as emotional as I do, but now that I have my own child, I can sense the pain she carried inside all those years."

KIM NGUYET LE

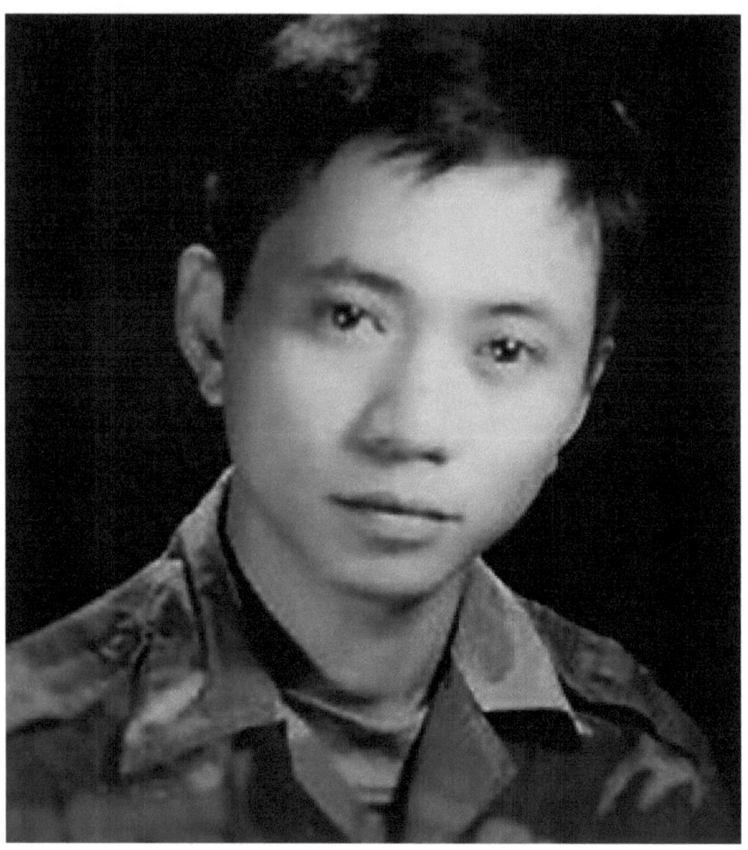

Portrait of Kiên Dương when he served in the Vietnamese Army.

"Our late father, Kiên Dương, fought in the Vietnamese Army until the very end–the Fall of Saigon. He risked everything on a dangerous journey by boat across the ocean to give his children a better life. He also spent his life helping hundreds of Vietnamese refugees to come to the US, providing housing if needed, helping them find jobs, and driving them to appointments. He was recognized as 'Volunteer of the Year' in our hometown of Beloit, Wisconsin, where we were sponsored by First Baptist Church and where my father lived until his passing in 2011. We are incredibly proud of his selflessness to help other Vietnamese to have a better life."

———————————————————

DƯƠNG THỦY (DUONG SHEAHAN)

John with his parents at School of Infantry, Camp Gieger, North Carolina. (November 2015)

"I was one of only two Vietnamese Marines in a company of over a hundred men. It was quite rare to find another Vietnamese Marine, especially in the Infantry, and when you did, it felt like running into a second cousin. Every Vietnamese Marine I met usually shared a similar family story—parents who pleaded with them to go to school and become doctors instead of joining the Marines, and the story of how their families had risked their lives to escape the war in Vietnam.

Without my family's bravery and sacrifices, I wouldn't be able to enjoy the life I live now. To this day, being an American-born Vietnamese in the military remains my life's proudest achievement. And even though my mom didn't exactly agree with me joining years ago, she now introduces me to her friends as her son in the Marines—not as an IT Technician."

JOHN HOANG

Amy M. Le with her cousin, Tri, in Seattle, WA after Amy wrote her first novel. (2019)

"When I wrote *Snow in Vietnam* and *Snow in Seattle*, my cousin, Tri, was my primary source on how we escaped. In 1976 he stopped going to school at age fourteen. We escaped Vietnam with my mother in 1979 out of Tra Vinh and ended up at the Galang Refugee Camp in Indonesia.

In 1980 we were sponsored to Seattle, Washington. Tri was almost eighteen, but my mom lied about his age by two years so that he could get an education. He dropped out of high school because learning English was too hard. He was terribly homesick and spiraled into a life of smoking, drinking, partying, and rebelling, only to find redemption later in life."

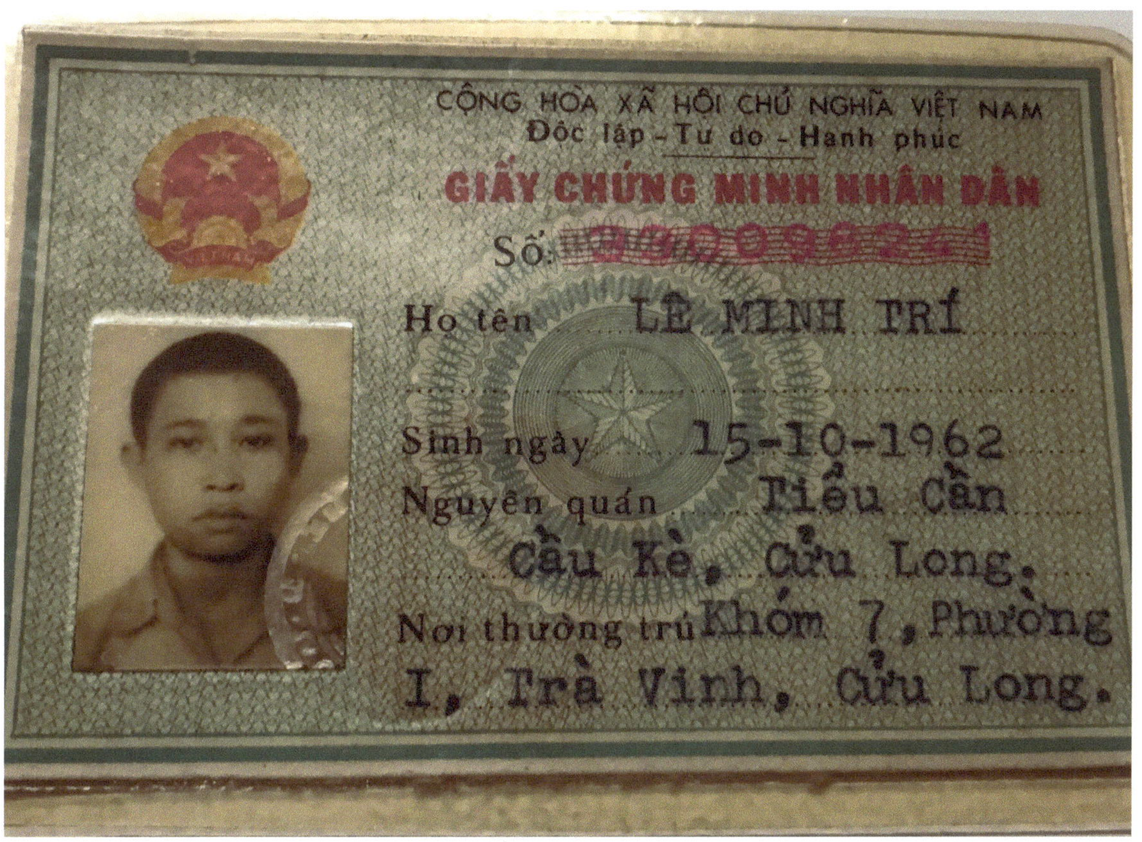

Le Minh Tri's new identification card issued in Tra Vinh, Vietnam, by the new government after the fall of Saigon. (November 1978)

"After the communist took over Saigon, they issued everyone new IDs. This one is from November 6, 1978, when my cousin was sixteen. It notes a scar above his brow as an identifying mark."

AMY M. LE

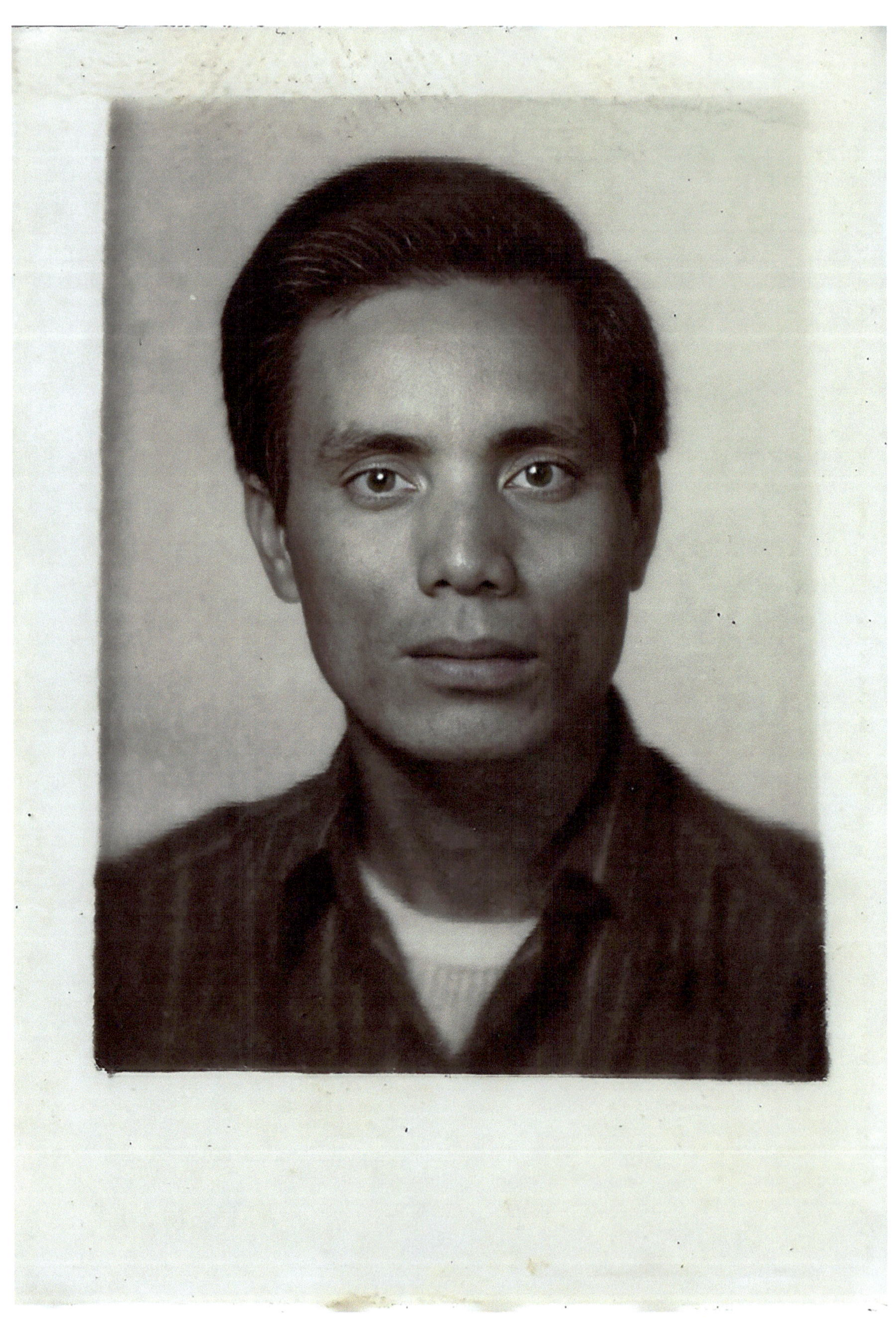

Alison's father, Com V. Nguyen

Com V. Nguyen mends a fishing net. (1981)

"My dad was a fisherman in Vietnam, so he became a fisherman in the U.S.. We settled in Panama City, FL, and he trawled for shrimp. He was one of many Vietnamese fishermen who worked in the Gulf of Mexico after the war. In his downtime, he would nhậu with his friends, drinking and unwinding from working long hours on their boats. He passed away suddenly at the age of thirty-seven. As an adult, I often reflect on how hard it must have been for him and my mom to leave behind everything they knew, to raise a family in a foreign land."

ALISON HỒNG NGUYỄN LIHALAKHA

Chau Pham wearing her daughter Alison's cap and gown at her law school graduation in Seattle, WA. (2001)

"In 1975, at the age of twenty-six, with three kids and her fourth child on the way, my mother applied for and was granted a microfinance loan to build a new fishing boat. Neither she nor the government bank could foresee that the boat would be our means of escape.

Fighting and unrest had spread from Sài Gòn to the villages, and her plan was to fill the boat with food and water to last several days. We would go out and stay at sea until the fighting in the nearby villages died down. Her idea to wait out the fighting was optimistic at best. Our family, and many others in our village, crammed onto the boat and escaped at the end of April. We were later picked up by a commercial ship, and our fishing boat had to be left behind.

Having only completed middle school, my mom wanted us to have all the opportunities she hadn't gotten. After my law school graduation ceremony, I insisted she put on my cap and gown for a photo. My law degree was as much her achievement as it was mine."

ALISON HỒNG NGUYỄN LIHALAKHA

"Our mother, Nguyet, projects a calm demeanor amidst chaos and uncertainty of the future. Her soft smile is indicative of a safe and secure vision of our future in America with our father, Oscar Baltazar. My parents were worried since there was little food and water for the four of us during our stay at the refugee camp. Our mom looks cool and lovely, despite the oppressive heat and humidity.

Being Amerasian presented an added layer of complexity with how I identified myself for most of my life. Society grouped me as either Caucasian or Hispanic (based on my dad's surname). Depending on certain situations, I was not white enough or brown enough to fit into certain groups, directly or indirectly. People simply refused to believe I was Asian."

———————————————

SANDY LIEN LAM GEOGHEGAN

Nguyet and her children at Clark Air Base in the Philippines. (1975)

Stylish Pair: Annie Ly's parents as a young couple in Olympia, WA. (1980)

"This is one of my favorite photos of my parents while they were still dating. Looking at it, I'm reminded of their life before me-young, child-free, and ever-so-stylish. If you didn't know them and their stories, you would never guess that they were still getting their bearings in a new country, learning a new language and culture, building a new life, missing family members who were still in Vietnam, and dealing with economic hardship after the war."

ANNIE LY

Young and Carefree: Tricia Vuong's parents as a young couple in California. (1980s)

"I recently discovered this photograph of my parents that I had never seen before. It was taken shortly after they arrived in America and reunited in California. I love how young and carefree they appear, almost as if they had not just come from a war-torn country, but were instead proud survivors trying to fit into their new home."

TRICIA VUONG

Nguyên Ngô (center with a green shirt) stands with his family at the Galang Refugee Camp in Indonesia. (1980)

Nguyên Ngô (first child on left) arriving with his family in the United States at Middletown, PA. (1981)

"My family arrived in the United States in 1981. This is us at Harrisburg International Airport. I am the boy on the left. Back then, I struggled with being a minority."

NGUYÊN NGÔ

Backyard family portrait after Vietnamese Sunday mass at St. Anthony's in Palacios, TX. (1997)

"Family photographs only happen for holidays, and it is rare to have one at home because our father, Hoang Van Nguyen, was typically the photographer. This photo was taken after Vietnamese mass at St. Anthony's, with Matthew wearing the Thiếu Nhi bandana and everyone in their Sunday best."

Sac Thi Dao prepares a meal to celebrate Christmas in California. (1985)

"My mother, Sac Thi Dao, has a few photos of herself from when she was younger. This portrait was taken after she graduated college and spent her second Christmas with our father. The two were visiting my father's extended family, who had just made their way to the United States and were celebrating their first Christmas here."

ANN NGUYEN

Loi Dang (second row) and a group of young boys and men standing in front of a residence at the Galang Refugee Camp in Indonesia. (July 1981)

"The summer of 1981 in the Galang camp was fun for my dad (Loi Dang). He stayed at Hawkins Road in Singapore before being moved to Galang. My dad is the one in the light grey pants. Ha Nguyen is the one in the yellow shirt. My dad often wonders where the other guys are who were on the boat with him. Their names are Tan, Khanh, and Dung."

NICOLE DOORN

"I didn't speak any English. It's tough for any age from 13 to 18. It's definitely a time where you feel very isolated. I remember learning English from the Brady Bunch. I felt so unstable. You still want someone to take care of you. And my parents were not with us. I was with my three brothers. It was a very lonely time."

YEN NGO
VAN DA
EPISODE 18
VIETNAMESE BOAT PEOPLE PODCAST

LISTEN HERE

"This was the only picture I saw of my father, Khoa Van Tran, taken in 1975 before he came to America. He was very proud of it because it made him look like a 'tough and cool guy.' He didn't have or share family photos with the kids. Then when he died, we found boxes hidden in a closet with papers and photos."

—————————

ANH TRAN NG

Hai Van Nguyen (left) and Lan Nguyen (right) experienced their first winter together in Minneapolis, Minnesota while they dated. (Thanksgiving 1975)

"My mom (Lan Nguyen) was sponsored by a family in Sauk Centre, Minnesota, and my dad (Hai Van Nguyen) was sponsored by a woman in Marshfield, Wisconsin. They met up at a friend's place in Minneapolis while they were courting to celebrate their first Thanksgiving in the United States. This was also their first ever winter and they were shocked by the snow and cold!"

Hai Van Nguyen (left) and Lan Nguyen (right) share a laugh a few months before marriage in Marshfield, Wisconsin. (1976)

"This was a few months before my parents got married. They took a trip to Marshfield, Wisconsin, to visit my dad's brothers, who were still living with their sponsor. For me (their daughter), this photo shows how happy they were despite the challenges of navigating a new country as young people."

KARENA NGUYEN

"Our biggest challenge was finding financial stability as Vietnamese immigrants in the United States. For many decades after coming to America in 1977, we lived in poverty.

My father, Tai Lu, and mother, Sang Nguyen Lu, eventually took a risk and became business owners. My father learned to become an electrician and fixed TVs and VCRs. My mother became a nail technician. Both leased a small business space with the front of the house being a nail shop and the back of the space being a TV/VCR repair shop.

This photo is of my parents and their four children seeing snow for the first time in Utah. My family arrived in America with little money and clothes. Coming from Vietnam to America, my older siblings did not know what to make of these 'tiny ice particles' they saw falling from the sky. We were grateful for the local church giving us winter clothes."

—————————————————————

KIM ANH LU

Tai Lu (father) and Sang Nguyen Lu (mother) with their children in Utah see snow for the first time. (1978)

A family dinner for Grandmother's birthday in Falls Church, VA. (1992)

"When you dig a little deeper, leaving behind an identity in Vietnam in many ways was the biggest challenge. My grandmother was a successful business woman - owned a movie theater - and came to America and washed dishes and cleaned restaurants. My uncle was a doctor who had to start a new career. My father and mother were entrepreneurs in their own rights and had to start over and become "new people" - cutting hair and working overnight shifts at convenience stores while they were getting their footing. Even though they've gone through so much, they live with joy and kindness."

RICHARD LUONG

Brothers, Ha Nguyen Vu (left) and Ha Tuan Anh (right), present to their adoptive parents on Christmas day in Morristown, NJ, a token of appreciation for their unwavering love and support throughout the years. (2019)

"Our parents in Vietnam (The Le Vu Family) made the ultimate sacrifice when they sent my brother and me out to sea as refugees in the '80s. It was not until we were lost at sea did my brother and I realize the magnitude of brotherhood. We made a promise to each other that no matter what happened to us, we would never separate. Vu was my beacon of hope. Our other brothers and sisters in Vietnam (eight of us altogether) were left behind.

We were adopted by the Parisi Family. I think one of the best highlights of my childhood was to bring my adoptive parents back to Vietnam to meet my biological parents and vice versa. We were indeed blessed to have the best of both worlds."

ANH PARISI (HA TUAN ANH)

"My father always made sure to take a lot of pictures in our childhood, which I've now come to truly appreciate. In America, my parents worked hard but Sundays were always reserved for family time. We'd eat in Chinatown and go shopping together. Our extended family also immigrated to Los Angeles so we had a sense of community around us.

My siblings and I had a very wonderful childhood in California, growing up near our families and cousins. Our lives were rooted in family and community, and that has stayed with us through adulthood. "

―――――――――――――――――――――――

KERRY LY

Kerry Ly (far right) with her siblings, Christopher Ly (front), Janet Ly (left), and Belinda Ly (middle) playing outside their apartment in Alhambra, California. (1987)

"The picture was taken in 1983 at Galang refugee camp Indonesia. My mom escaped with four kids on a boat, and after a crazy 5-day journey, we ended up at the first island. Galang was the fourth and last one. The top picture was taken on the day we were interviewed and accepted for resettlement to the US. At the interview, my mom was asked only one question: "How can you expect to take care of four kids by yourself in America with no husband?" (My dad was a POW when we escaped). My mom answered, "I have these two hands. I've taken them this far. I sure can take care of them again." The US representative was so impressed that he accepted us right away.

Fast forward to the picture on the bottom, taken on Thanksgiving 2024, forty-one years later. My mom raised us and took care of us while working three jobs in America. All four of us went to college. My sister is a pharmacist. I'm an attorney. One of the younger twin brothers is an optometrist. The other one is in IT. We sponsored my dad in 1989, which was the first time I ever met him, when I was sixteen years old. I was two when he was taken away in 1975."

———————————————————————

DUC TRAN

From refugee camp to now, Duc Tran and his family recreate their photo from 1983 to 2024.

Paulina Vo's 4th grade school photo.

My sister was proud,

because her house didn't smell like fish sauce.

I lived with her so I did too, because we both knew,

kids in school were cruel,

to them, smelling different was easy to use.

But, my eye shape gave me away anyway.

How could I tell my parents?

They packed only what they could hold,

trekked through jungles, waded in water,

with someone else's sons and daughters,

and a sea of families,

waiting on an island for saving.

Yet here I was,

20 years later embarrassed because,

mẹ's thịt kho was too pungent.

I loved it, and at the same time ran far from it.

I fought hard against myself for years

ignoring my language,

wishing I wasn't Asian.

I'd push the tip of my nose up just a little in the mirror,

dreaming of waking up a different color,

a different body,

with different eyes,

change how everyone else saw me.

PAULINA VO

"In the span of sixty years, my dad's life changed from surviving a boat journey to moving to America. However, some things stay the same. The Saigon Zoo is still here for the two of us to enjoy."

———————————————————

MEGGIE TRAN

Meggie Tran's dad, Thien Tran, as a toddler with his grandmother at the Saigon Zoo in Saigon, Vietnam. (early 1960s)

Meggie Tran with her dad, Thien Tran, at the Saigon Zoo in HCMC, Vietnam. (2023)

Nora Nguyen with her mother outside Samford University in Birmingham, Alabama. (1983)

"On the night that my mom and I fled in 1978, I was sick. By the time we got to our ship, my mom fainted. We ended up in a refugee camp in Hong Kong, then arrived in San Jose, CA in 1979. Starting over in a new country with very little money was extremely challenging. My mom signed up for English language classes and studied for a certificate to be an electronic technician at a local community college. A few years later, we moved to Birmingham, Alabama so that she could study to be a pharmacist, which was her profession in Vietnam.

This is us at Samford University, where my mom attended pharmacy school. We lived in Birmingham, Alabama when I was in third through eighth grade."

NORA NGUYEN

"My mother worked at an American military base in Da Nang where she met my father who was stationed there. After I was born, my mother took me to the Sacred Heart Orphanage in Da Nang. After ten months, I was adopted by an American family and raised in California.

Growing up as the bi-racial (half-Black & half-Vietnamese) adopted son of Swedish & Irish parents was a constant test of identity. My adolescence was confusing, challenging, and fascinating all at the same time. Those adolescent years were also painful as I sought acceptance from the various cultural traditions represented in me. Eventually, I learned that my difference could be a good thing.

The top picture was taken during the ten months I lived at Sacred Heart Orphanage. It was sent to my adoptive family while my paperwork was being completed. This was the moment they laid eyes on their new child for the first time. The Catholic nun holding me is Sr. Marie Martine. The bottom photo was taken when I returned to Da Nang in 1998 with my adoptive family, and we reconnected with Sr. Martine!"

CANH OXELSON

At the Sacred Heart Orphanage in Da Nang, Vietnam. (1972)

A Reunion: Canh Oxelson returns to the Sacred Heart Orphanage in Da Nang, Vietnam. (1988)

Rosalie Lam's sister, Grace Praso, wore this custom ao dai wedding dress that was made in Saigon. (1969)

"My sister, Grace Praso, was in Japan in 1968. She wore this áo dài when she got married at the Vietnamese Embassy in Tokyo, Japan in 1969. Grace was not able to come home for the wedding because of the war going on in Saigon. We had the dress made and sent it to her. Far away from home, with no relatives and parents, my sister, and her late husband, Michael, got married at the Vietnamese Embassy in Tokyo. They were warmly received at the Embassy and she still vividly remembers that her ao dai was highly praised."

ROSALIE LAM

"I remember having friends over in our house and I would just make sure that our house doesn't smell a certain way, that it doesn't smell like nước mắm [fish sauce]. Like making sure that when my friends come in, they don't see my mom like karaoke at night or like watching cải lương or Paris by Night. You know, I just don't want to have to explain to them."

VI SON TRINH
SECOND GEN
EPISODE 24
VIETNAMESE BOAT PEOPLE PODCAST

LISTEN HERE

Intergenerational
Impact and
Moving Forward

Through each word, the silence breaks,
A bridge rebuilt, a past embraced.
Honoring those who came before,
We heal, remember, and restore.

"I have a greater sense of myself through having explored their stories and who they were and they are. In some ways, I'm able to pinpoint, like, this thing that they're saying to me isn't personal. It's not with the intention to hurt me."

"My mother (Nguyễn Thị Liễu) was born into a prominent family as one of twelve children. She grew up surrounded by the finer things in life, but within a strict household where image and reputation weighed heavily on her shoulders. Her mother was a savvy businesswoman, ahead of her time. Her father was a principled and charismatic leader, a high-ranking officer during the French colonial era in Vietnam. Her bond with her father was so profound that it's still remembered and spoken of with reverence among our relatives. His sudden death, just before civil war consumed the country, left a wound in her that never fully healed.

Yet even in grief, she pressed on. In the final months before the Fall of Sài Gòn, everything her family built unraveled. Just three days after giving birth to my older sister, her sixth child, my mother and father fled their home in Đà Nẵng in chaos with their children. They found refuge in Nha Trang, and thirty days later, Sài Gòn fell. My mother lost everything she owned—everything her parents worked so hard to build. The life she once knew vanished."

———————————

TRACEY NGUYỄN MANG

Tracey's maternal grandfather, Nguyễn Trâm (1906-1967), in his home office in Vietnam, year unknown.

"The years after 1975 were filled with hardship
—never enough food to feed the children, and
constant fear under the new regime. My
mother was selling goods on the black market
and secretly mapping out multiple escape
routes for different families, including ours.
By the time she turned forty, she was starting
over yet again in America, with nothing—
raising seven children, working odd jobs to
make ends meet, and still finding ways to
slowly repay the debt owed to the people who
had given us passage to freedom. Throughout
my childhood, I remember my mother
welcoming or sponsoring many refugees into
our small home—relatives, even distant ones—
anyone who needed a place to stay until they
could find their footing.

It's hard to believe how serene and carefree
my mother looks in this photo—just 15 or 16 at
the time, with her whole life ahead of her.
Instead, she had to fight for survival for most
of her adult life. I look at this photo now and
wonder if she knew then just how much
strength her future would demand. It's the
kind of strength I hope lives on in me—and
someday, in my children."

TRACEY NGUYỄN MANG

Nguyễn Thị Liễu (Tracey's mom) in Vietnam. (1957)

"My cousin in Vietnam sent me this photo of my grandparents. My grandfather died just before I was born. My grandma suffered a stroke shortly after and was paralyzed on her left side. Their swagger wasn't something I was able to experience, but it's crazy how much my dad and I look like my grandpa. Now I know where I got my swag from!"

LISA TRAN

Lisa Tran's grandparents in Saigon.

"My father (Christopher Vũ Văn Hiển) carried in his heart the weight of a lost homeland and the hope for a brighter future for his newborn son. He navigated a new world with resilience and quiet determination, always putting his family before himself. Though he is gone, the profound love and sacrifices he made resonate deeply within me, shaping the person I am today. His enduring spirit will forever be my guiding light.

This old photo of us kids with our vibrant áo dài is a stark reminder of our diasporic childhood and now feels bittersweet. We were a testament to our family's attempt to hold onto tradition amidst a new world. It's a jarring contrast to see us young, poised, and innocent. Lined up from smallest to tallest are sister Jackie, cousin Melanie, brother Henry, and cousin Thy, who tragically is no longer with us to share in adulthood's complexities. I'm in the far right in dark blue. This photo is a precious reminder of innocence, growth, loss, and the experiences binding us together."

TONY SAIMASTON VŨ

Children celebrating their Vietnamese heritage wearing vibrant áo dài clothes. (From left to right: Jackie, Melanie, Henry, Thy, and Tony Vu)

Ha Phung and his daughter, An, at the Pulau Tengah refugee camp in Malaysia. He is standing next to the boat where his wife gave birth to their daughter. (1979)

"I keep this photo in a frame at home as a reminder of my roots. Although my father and I are estranged now, seeing it on my shelf brings a sense of connection to him and our shared past. My father's smile in this photo radiates a hope that, over time, I saw give way to the weight of his experiences. His excitement for a fresh start in America slowly faded, replaced by fear and insecurity as he struggled to adjust to a new life, carrying the memories and traumas of our past."

———————————————

AN PHUNG

"This photo touches me. Our family's story has always been told with sadness and the intensity of the experiences of war. It was not a normal time in my parents' lives, and yet I feel I have only known my parents from this point in their lives. This photo, for me, is a moment where I see them not from the perspective of war, but from a glimpse of safety, sharing a moment of laughter with one another, and sensing a future without war. I don't get to see my parents in these moments together often, so it reminds me of the innocence and hope they must have once had together."

THUY M. PHAM

Thuy M. Pham's parents in Alabama. (1976)

Mary Nhin and her mom, Carol Nguyen Gaston in
Texarkana, TX. (1977)

They left with the stars as their guide,

A battered boat on a merciless tide.

Through dark waters and skies of gray,

They sailed for hope, for dreams, and a better day.

But love was their anchor, courage their sail,

In a sea of despair, they dare not fail.

A camp became their refuge of dreams,

A place where nothing was as it seems.

Yet, from that soil of struggle and strife,

They planted the seeds for a better life.

America, a land of promise untold,

Its streets were not paved with glittering gold.

But with calloused hands and sleepless nights,
They carved a path through endless fights.
From sweat and tears, they paved my way,
So I could stand where I am today.

A builder of dreams, a teller of tales,
An entrepreneur whose vision sails.
Four million hearts, young and true,
Have felt the light of what I do.

But it's my parents' journey, their fight, their fire,
That lifts me up, that takes me higher.
Their story whispers throughout all I've done -
A legacy that will be passed to my son.

Their ocean crossed, their dreams in hand,
Now ripple out across this land.
My parents crossed the ocean so I could reach the stars,
Their journey etched in my soul, their strength in my scars.

For every step I take, every dream I dare,
I honor the courage that brought me here.

MARY NHIN

Portrait of young Trần Diệu Hằng in Saigon, Vietnam.

"On the day Saigon fell, my mom had only a few minutes to grab whatever she could from her home because she had to leave immediately. This is one of the photos she managed to take with her."

———————————————

TRỊNH VY UYÊN (CINDY TRINH)

Han's mom, Diep Thi Thanh Nguyen, in Westminster, California.
(1995)

"My mom took pictures to send back to my aunt. She always looked so beautiful and dressed up for these photos. I think it was a way of sharing reassurance that we lived a good life here. At the time when we all lived together, we were living okay. When we were forced to leave this house, we experienced a lot of economic struggle. I remember growing up really poor but looking at this picture gives a different feeling."

Diep Thi Thanh Nguyen with her baby, Han, who was born in the Philippines Processing Center (PRPC). (1991)

"I was the first one of my family born in the Philippines Refugee Camp. I think about how the stories of the refugee camp often depict poor dehumanizing stories. When I look at this picture, it was a celebration of life (of me)."

HAN NGUYỄN

Photo by Brandon Nguyen while on vacation in Vietnam at one of the many caves in the Marble Mountains in Ngũ Hành Sơn, near Đà Nẵng, Vietnam. (2018)

"The word việt kiều means 'Overseas Vietnamese' according to Google Translate, but the word carries many layered connotations depending on who is saying it and who it is targeted at.

I hope that one day, the word việt kiều no longer carries negative connotations for me. I hope that one day, việt kiều doesn't just mean overseas Vietnamese when a native sees me. Instead, I hope it captures the love I have for Vietnam, its traditions, its food, its language, and its people.

I hope that one day, việt kiều will be a term welcoming us home and not a reminder of why we left. I hope that one day they will recognize the love and respect I have for a country I never lived in."

BRANDON NGUYEN

Ashlee Newcomb's bà nội (paternal grandmother) holding
Ashlee's daughter (her first great grandchild) in Orlando, FL.
(2021)

"Being half-Vietnamese, I feel a deep sense of gratitude for my family's sacrifices and the cultural foundation they've provided. It's truly magical to think that my grandparents, who experienced so much, now have a great-grandchild. Their resilience and care have shaped my life in ways I'll never fully grasp, and I'm in awe of how our family's journey has come full circle. Every day, I honor their strength, their sacrifices, and the legacy they've created."

ASHLEE NEWCOMB

"Since childhood, my uncle from New Orleans has always visited my family in San Jose. As he ages, I've become more curious about his stories. He spent four years in the Vietnam War and four years in a reeducation camp. After he was released, he escaped Vietnam and came to New Orleans in 1982. He was then able to sponsor other family members, including my dad, who arrived in 1992."

Alexander Nguyễn visits with his uncle, Chú Thịnh, in New Orleans, LA. (February 2024)

ALEXANDER NGUYỄN

"The top photo in black and white was taken of my grandparents before my grandad went to war. The bottom photo are of my grandparents on their 50th wedding anniversary.

My family's history is steeped in resilience and sacrifice, beginning with my ancestor from four generations ago, Saint Michael Hồ Đình Hy. As the last high-ranking official executed under the Nguyễn dynasty for his Christian faith, his unwavering conviction left an indelible mark on our family's values.

Continuing this legacy of perseverance, my grandfather served valiantly in the Vietnam War, only to be captured when his plane was shot down. He endured 13 years of imprisonment, a testament to his unbreakable spirit.

Meanwhile, my grandmother held the family together, raising eight children by selling diamonds to make ends meet. At just 15 years old, my father—her eldest—stepped up as a father-figure, shouldering responsibilities far beyond his years.

Now, more than 50 years since the war ended, my family's journey is nothing short of extraordinary. We've built a legacy of resilience and strength that continues to inspire future generations."

MICHAEL ĐÌNH HỒ

Ông bà Hồ Đình Dương&Thông (1969)

"In front of their childhood home together for the very first time in forty-seven years, my mother and her sister moved carefully and slowly, tip-toeing as if they were transported back to that early morning in March 1978 when they had to quietly escape. Uncertain of what the next moment would present them with, they discreetly motioned goodbye to their mother who was looking down from their balcony witnessing her three daughters blend into the darkness, along with their youth and their innocence, not knowing what they might face and if that would be the last sight she would have of them."

———————————————————

CAROLYN ANH VAN

Two sisters return to their childhood home on Ha Ton Quyen Street in District 11 (formally District 5) in Saigon, Vietnam. (March 2024)

"I created this family portrait to commemorate the Vietnam War's 45th anniversary in 2020 and reflect on the richness of my family history, which includes Amerasians, South Asians (Indian/Pakistani) in Vietnam, and Vietnamese in America. The setting is Milton Lee Olive Park in Chicago, which is dedicated to a Black Vietnam War veteran. In the background is the John Hancock Center, a skyscraper that was built during the peak of the war in 1969. As a result of that very war, my relatives became refugees and settled in Chicago in the 1980s. Since Vietnam War memorials in the U.S. usually neglect Vietnamese subjectivity, I treated this park as a backdrop, and in doing so, the portrait captures multiple layers of history."

RICHARD GESSERT

Richard Gessert's family portrait in Olive Park, Chicago, IL, representing the multiple layers of history and the richness of a diverse family. (2019)

Phuong Tran's Bà Ngoại (maternal grandmother), Vinh Thi Trương, preparing dessert in Alhambra, Los Angeles, CA. (1979)

"Bà Ngoại making rau câu in her home kitchen. I think about the lineage of this artistic practice, which was passed onto me by my mother and passed on to her from her mother. I've always felt both of their divine spirits in me when I cook."

PHUONG TRAN

"I remembered that they were supposed to have an interpreter that day with the appointment, but there was some type of mix-up, so there was no interpreter. So I had to be both daughter and interpreter that day. And when the neurologist explained the diagnosis, I remember looking at my mom and my dad, who was looking at me to explain things. My heart just fell to my stomach."

"My father fought for South Vietnam for about five years: 18 months in the military academy and three years as a second lieutenant with a platoon in Quảng Nam province in Central Vietnam. After South Vietnam fell to the Communist North in 1975, he was captured and imprisoned in Trại học tập cải tạo—detention camps run by the North Vietnamese in the jungles of Central Vietnam. He was sentenced to three years and subjected to back-breaking labor, minimal food, and violent treatment as a means of revenge and indoctrination into the new government's principles.

My father ran away from the Vietnamese Communist government, away from the horrors of warfare, so that my sister and I could lead better lives. So, I ran with him, but I kept running... away from him, my home, and now seemingly from myself. I've skimmed through every region of the US in temporary living situations, never lasting more than two years. I have a mysterious urge to traverse the world alone, taking myself to dangerous situations in Africa, the Middle East, and South America to find something. That something always seems to be missing. I find myself now in New York City, a city that is finally big enough for me to keep running... running to find something to heal my inability to connect, lost somewhere at sea among the boats that carried my family to escape."

———————————————————————

TRACY DONG

Dang Han Dong's uniform. Photo taken by Tracy in Surrey, British Columbia, Canada. (December 2021)

Thi's father, Đoàn Văn Úc and mother Đoàn Thị Điệp, in a refugee camp in Malaysia. (1979)

"After my dad's release from the reeducation (labor) camp in Viet Nam, my mom was able to sneak him gold to secure him a spot on a boat to escape Viet Nam in search of freedom and a better life. Though afforded this slim opportunity for escape, his answer to my mom was, 'I won't go unless you come with me.'

They built a life and family together in the U.S. and transformed adversity into the American dream. They were met with a different trial in their golden years: dementia had found my mom. Their love for each other is very heartwarming. At a recent medical appointment for my mom, as I was filling out her paperwork, I noticed out of the corner of my eye a subtle movement with my parents who were sitting silently next to me in the waiting room. They sat still, not saying anything. My mom stared ahead with her now usual, blank look. I noticed my dad silently reach his hand over into her space and rest his hand on her arm. To any observer, it may look like he was trying to provide her some comfort through that small, tender act, but I wonder if it was also to provide him comfort. That perhaps small touches like this is how they create the bridge in the midst of war, an ocean, or a dying mind to always find each other."

THI ĐOÀN

Just Married: Mai Tran (bride) and On Tran (groom) on their wedding day in Rạch Giá, Vietnam. (May 8, 1965)

"This is a photo of my maternal grandparents at their wedding reception in Rạch Giá, Vietnam. Looking at this, it's hard not to think about how they had no idea what the future held. They'd soon have five kids, and their journey would take them far from their homeland. In 2025, they'll celebrate their 60th wedding anniversary."

KELLY PRISBREY

Le Thi Hanh poses in front of a mirror in San Diego, California. (1977)

"My mother is the strongest woman I have ever known. What she lived through by the time she was twenty-five takes my breath away when I reflect where I was and what I was doing at the same age. Despite the challenges of a new life in an often inhospitable foreign land with four kids (ages five and younger), she never let the hardships show. Mama was just a little girl who wore big pants. This is one of my favorite photos of her. She always wore her ao dai in America. I am so proud of this woman."

LƯU TRỌNG ĐẠ THẢO (TINA LƯU)

183

"After forty-two years, I went back to Vietnam and saw the home I grew up in. Only a few walls are still standing. I will never forget the beautiful memories. It was impossible to contain my tears. My daughter was with me. It was her first visit to Vietnam and to see and understand the Vietnamese diaspora made her appreciate and feel grateful for the life she has now."

LEN TRAN

Len Tran and his daughter, Lara, stand in front of a replica of the boat that took twenty five Vietnamese out to sea for twenty one days.

Len Tran's family home in Vietnam that he left behind in 1982 and its condition in 2024.

De Nguyen's parents on their wedding day. (1970)

De Nguyen (in front center at age 5) with his family and relatives visiting their new home's capital in Washington, DC. (1980)

"My biggest challenge was assimilating to a new culture and language, while my parents struggled to provide for our entire family. What I'm most proud of are the sacrifices they made and the successful life they built for all of us."

DE NGUYEN

A UNHCR identification card of Lee Mei Wan and her daughter, Ngoc Dep Tran, in Malaysia. Lee was six months pregnant with her third child at the time. (1979)

"The arrival of the Red Khmer was the final drop to leave. We lived nearby Chau-Doc. After several horrible wars, they tried again to live a peaceful life. My father was struggling with the communist government and wanted to have a stable and good life for his family so we fled Vietnam. My parents had no one helping them.

Because of their sacrifices, they are living a happy life in the Netherlands with their three daughters. Unfortunately, their eldest and only son passed at age sixteen in 1989."

NGOC DEP TRAN

Tung Nguyen (middle) hugging her mother, Sua, and brother Lai. (1993)

"It took three days and four different airports to reach Đà Nẵng. When I walked out of customs, I looked through the glass doors and saw my mother standing in the middle of a group of her grandchildren. She looked so old. So skinny. So tired. Our eyes locked, and I started to cry. How had she survived all these years while I was away? How did she take care of all these children? How had she kept the family together? As soon as I reached her, my mother grabbed me into a hug. My brother, Lai, came up from behind her. The three of us held each other and cried. 'I'm sorry,' I choked through my tears."

TUNG NGUYEN

“In the photo, my mother is in the center, flanked by my grandmother and father. It was taken on her wedding day right in front of my paternal grandfather's house. My mother is one of the strongest people I know, and I love this photo because it highlights her presence.

The look in my mom's eyes captures her strength, courage, and resilience, serving as a constant reminder of these qualities. It symbolizes the love and support that have shaped our family.”

ANH DUC NGUYEN-JANZEN

Anh Duc Nguyen-Janzen's mother on her wedding day in Vietnam. (1967)

Bella Nguyen's parents and grandparents outside their home in Louisiana.

"My ông bà ngoại (maternal grandparents) settled in Louisiana after arriving in America, and this photo was taken outside their home—a place that came to symbolize their triumphs, survival, and new beginnings. My ông ngoại, holding me here, passed away when I was 17, while my bà ngoại recently became a centenarian. This photo feels like a bridge between generations—a reminder of resilience, love, and the passage of time, especially now that I am the same age my parents were when this moment was captured."

BELLA NGUYEN

Anh Duc Nguyen-Janzen's father, the photographer, in the refugee camp in the Philippines. (1981)

"In the photo, my father is seen holding a camera. He began working in a photo lab for his uncle at the age of seven. While in the refugee camp in the Philippines, he borrowed a broken camera and took many passport and wedding photos for people there. His photography helped him earn enough to buy us a better place in the camp and even save $3,000 to bring with him to Germany. His passion for photography is the reason we have so many cherished memories."

ANH DUC NGUYEN-JANZEN

"My dad wanted to recreate the flavors of his childhood in Saigon but couldn't find a fish sauce that tasted like home. So in 2011, he decided that he would make it — and started Red Boat Fish Sauce. He left his job as an Apple engineer to recreate his memories of an intensely fragrant and umami-rich fish sauce. Today I am so proud to be the second generation of our family-owned business."

———————————————————

TIFFANY PHAM

Ann and Cuong Pham when they were first exploring the idea of bringing Phu Quoc fish sauce to the United States. (2006)

Ann and Cuong Pham with their children shortly after moving to their new house in Pleasanton, California. (1998)

Quang Vu Ha (second from right) with his dad at at the Sungei Besi Refugee Camp in Malaysia. (1983)

"My dad was part of the Vietnam People's Air Force (Không quân nhân dân Việt Nam). It was challenging growing up separated from my siblings and mom, and having a single father who struggled to adapt and provide for his family while learning to adjust to a new country and language. I was three years old when we left, with no memories of the refugee camp besides this photo. This is a cherished photo of mine that my dad was able to preserve from our boat journey with 49 other passengers escaping Vietnam. We were rescued after five days at sea and arrived in Malaysia. After six months in the camp, we would eventually be sponsored and accepted as refugees in Canada. It is one of the very few pictures of me as a child, and now, with my son being a similar age in 2024, it means more to me than ever."

QUANG VU HA

Samantha Vu (front row, age 3) at the refugee camp in Songkhla, Thailand, Tent 22, with her family. From left to right: Duc David Nguyen (uncle), Thanh Ha Nguyen (mom) holding Samantha's newborn sister, Uyen Ngoc Vu (dad), and Minh (family friend).

"We immigrated to America in 1980, and two years later, my other uncle came. There were six people in this little one bedroom apartment, where my dad later invited other Vietnamese immigrants who came. I had people whom I called uncle, but they weren't really my uncles. My dad said, "Well, we made it. We're still receiving help, but we can help others while we're still receiving help." That resonated with me. To this day, when the community gets together, I try as much as possible to do the same. We opened our home to lots of strangers coming to the United States seeking refuge, safety, and opportunity."

SAMANTHA VU TRAN

Vương Quang Tí was a bodybuilder in Vietnam and served in the South Vietnamese Army. (1950s)

"My father was a highly educated street rat-that's how he described himself. He was born in the year of the rat. After witnessing a horrific crime against his mother, he ran away from home at the age of ten and studied under the street lamps. He later won a scholarship to study in America and then came back to Vietnam to fight against the communists. One of his roles was to serve as bodyguard and chauffeur for the generals and their wives. Having witnessed many atrocities and committed violent aggressions against the VC, my father suffers extreme guilt and severe PTSD every day."

AMY M. LE

Mark F. Erickson (Đỗ Văn Hùng), seated center, with his Vietnamese family in Saigon. (2023)

"In April 1975, the American government evacuated over 2,500 children from Vietnam during Operation Babylift. The children were then adopted in America and other countries. I was two years old. This is the only photo I have of myself as a child. In 2023, I met my Vietnamese family for the first time in Saigon."

MARK F. ERICKSON (ĐỖ VĂN HÙNG)

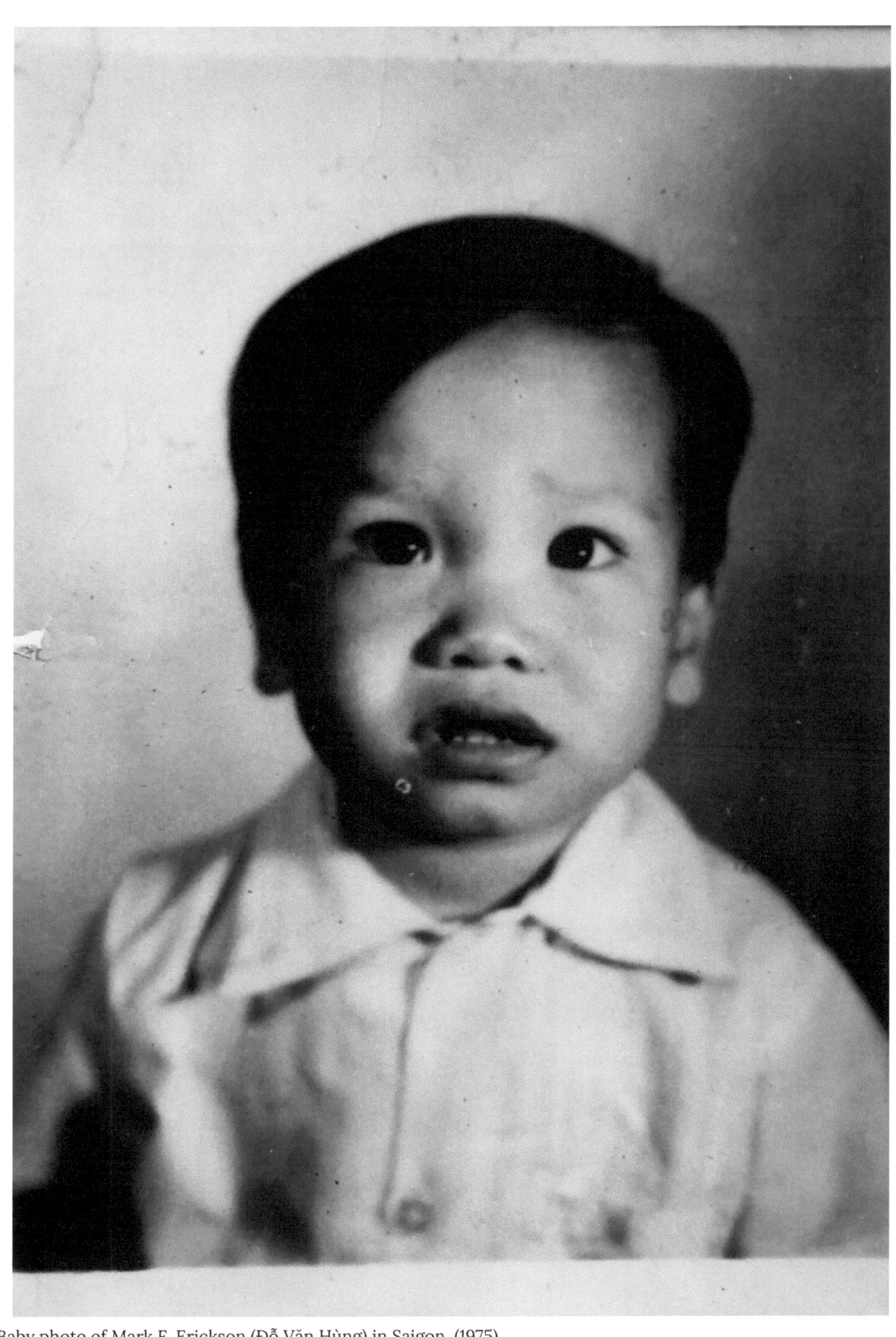

Baby photo of Mark F. Erickson (Đỗ Văn Hùng) in Saigon. (1975)

"My father's ID says he was born in 1939, but I recently discovered he was born in 1937. At the time, Vietnam was under French colonial rule as part of French Indochina. By 1940, Japanese forces had invaded the north, and within a year, their control extended across the central and southern regions—including the area near Nha Trang, where my father was born.

When he was around four years old, his entire village fled into the mountains to escape the war. They stayed hidden for nearly two years. By the time they returned in 1943, the farmlands were destroyed. My father was six by then, but had missed two years of schooling. With identification papers lost in the destruction, his parents lied about his birth year—claiming 1939—so he could start school from the beginning. That small lie became a permanent fact of his identity.

I love this photo of my parents—young, cool, and calm, as if war weren't unfolding around them. He met my mom when they were both in high school. Today, my father is living with dementia. Some days are good—he recalls his childhood in vivid detail, or tells me stories of how he courted Mom. On others, he forgets the month or how he got there. I find myself loving him more now than I ever did as a child. We were once distant, bound by silence. Perhaps I feared him. Perhaps he didn't know how to show love. But now, none of that matters. What matters are the moments we still share, even if the timeline blurs."

TRACEY NGUYỄN MANG

Nguyễn Hoàng Sanh and Nguyễn Thị Liễu, Tracey's parents Vietnam, year unknown.

The family reunites with the Vineville United Methodist Church in Macon, GA that sponsored them from Vietnam twenty-seven years prior. (May 24, 2008)

"Vineville United Methodist Church stands as a testament to the unwavering kindness and generosity that made our transition possible. This church played a pivotal role in sponsoring and welcoming eleven members of our family, helping us find not only a new home but also a sense of belonging. We will always carry deep gratitude for their compassion and generosity, which transformed our lives in ways we will never forget."

LOAN TRAN

"I wanted to understand why my mother gave me up. Like, what did she go through? And on my birthday, does she remember me? And I think she does, because I feel her energy. I feel her praying for me."

NAOKO TSUNODA (MỸ THỊ BÙI)
MỸ THỊ BÙI
EPISODE 30
VIETNAMESE BOAT PEOPLE PODCAST

LISTEN HERE

Share Your Story

We invite you to share your story through various mediums, such as interviews, short essays, or other formats on the VBP Journeys Map, a digital collective on our website. This collective is designed to embrace and honor all personal narratives. Together, we can paint a more comprehensive picture of the intricate and multifaceted experiences within the Vietnamese diaspora community.

To share your story, visit www.vietnameseboatpeople.org/journeys.

Acknowledgements

It has long been a dream of mine to create a book that captures the personal narratives of our Vietnamese diaspora community—stories told in a simple, sincere, and deeply moving way. I am endlessly grateful for all those who have helped Vietnamese Boat People grow into the organization it is today and for the many who supported this anthology from the spark of an idea to the pages in your hands.

To Amy M. Le and Alison Hồng Nguyễn Lihalakha—thank you for your unwavering support, sisterhood, and the many late nights spent editing and refining each story. Your thoughtful care in reviewing every narrative submission, and the time you spent connecting with storytellers to ensure authenticity and accuracy, were labors of love that elevated this collection.

To Anthony W. Nguyễn, who stepped in to create a stunning illustration of Vietnam's national flower, the lotus. Your art beautifully evokes the serenity and resilience of our people—rising with grace from the depths of trauma and turmoil. It perfectly encapsulates the spirit of this book.

To Katrina Schroeder, our talented book designer—thank you for your patience and artistry in shaping the layout of this anthology. You ensured that even the briefest stories made a lasting visual and emotional impact.

To Sophia Ma—thank you for helping launch our open call for photographs. Your care in reviewing each one to curate our powerful visual exhibition brought another layer of storytelling to this project.

There are so many others whose support and contributions have helped the overall mission of Vietnamese Boat People.

To our dedicated volunteers—Ashlee Newcomb, Bella Nguyen, Saoli Nguyen, Tricia Vuong, and Matt Young—thank you for being with me since the earliest days of VBP, helping turn a personal project into something larger for our community. To Nancy Le Blair, Lauren Nguyen, and Ben Nguyen—your behind-the-scenes work keeps our mission running strong. And to Brian Hoang, who continually lends his creative talents and brings beauty to our projects.

To our board members, past and present—Mark Erickson, Alison Hồng Nguyễn Lihalakha, Amy M. Le, Richard Luong, Thuan "Toon" Nguyen, Anh Parisi, and Len Tran—and to all the storytellers, volunteers, donors, and advocates of Vietnamese Boat People: thank you for your support, passion, and dedication to our collective mission. You've shown me that building community—and a team that feels like family—is the most important fuel we need to keep growing.

And last but never least, my partner, Jason Mang—thank you for always supporting my dreams and purpose, no matter how big or small. With your love, patience, and steady presence, I am constantly reminded that purpose and impact are not measured by size or scale, but by the hearts we touch.

Editors

Editor:

Tracey Nguyễn Mang is the founder of the Vietnamese Boat People (VBP) organization and the executive producer of its award-winning podcast. She is actively involved in various community and philanthropic efforts and serves on the Board of Trustees for the New Jersey Council for the Humanities. Prior to starting VBP, Tracey spent over twenty years in the corporate sector, with a focus on strategy, digital experiences, and corporate social responsibility. She frequently speaks on topics including storytelling, podcasting, Asian American narratives, community building, and social impact. She is also a licensed real estate professional in New Jersey and lives in Montclair with her husband, two kids, and their beloved dog.

Co-Editor:

Alison Hồng Nguyễn Lihalakha is the author of the award-winning coming-of-age memoir, *Salted Plums*, and a dual-language children's book, *ABCs of Arabia*. She was born in Vietnam and grew up in Florida and Kansas before heading off to explore the world. Alison spent over a decade living abroad with her husband and children. In Tunisia, Saudi Arabia, and most recently, South Korea, she made friends and explored new customs and cultures while sharing her own. Alison resides in Hawai'i, where she finds that local foods, lei-making, and the fresh tropical air are perfect for soothing the soul.

Copy Editor:

Amy M. Le is the founder of Quill Hawk Publishing (QHP), an Asian American, woman-owned hybrid publishing company dedicated to amplifying diverse voices one story at a time. She is the award-winning author of *The Snow Trilogy*, a series of auto-fiction novels based on her family's journey from Vietnam to America. When Amy is not writing, speaking, or publishing books, she devotes her time to volunteering and fundraising for organizations that speak to her heart. Born with a congenital heart defect, Amy also advocates for the CHD community through The Heart Community Collection, an online resource for heart warriors and their families. A Seattle-lite at heart, Amy currently resides in Edmond, OK, with her husband, son, and a revolving door of pets.

Art Illustrator:

Anthony W. Nguyễn is a multifaceted artist whose work emerges from the intersection of technology, storytelling, and creativity. Born in Honolulu, Hawai'i to Vietnamese immigrants, he brings a unique perspective shaped by his heritage and upbringing. While building a career as a software engineer, he continues to nurture his artistic vision, transforming personal experiences and emotional depth into visual expressions through paintings and illustrations. He currently resides in the Bay Area with his wife and growing family.

Vietnamese Boat People
a 501(c)3 nonprofit organization
Montclair, NJ
EIN: 83-1411011
To make a tax-deductible donation
visit www.vietnameseboatpeople.org/donate